ON POWER

ON POWER

A Philosophical Dialogue

Nicholas J. Pappas

Algora Publishing
New York

Library of Congress Cataloging-in-Publication Data —

Library of Congress Cataloging-in-Publication Data

Names: Pappas, Nicholas J., author.
Title: On power : a philosophical dialogue / Nicholas J. Pappas.
Description: New York : Algora Publishing, 2019.
Identifiers: LCCN 2019020173 (print) | ISBN 9781628943924 (soft cover :
    alk. paper) | ISBN 9781628943931 (hard cover : alk. paper)
Subjects: LCSH: Power (Philosophy)
Classification: LCC BD438 .P37 2019 (print) | LCC BD438 (ebook) | DDC
    320.01/1--dc23
LC record available at https://lccn.loc.gov/2019020173
LC ebook record available at https://lccn.loc.gov/2019981606

Printed in the United States

Table of Contents

INTRODUCTION   1

THE DIALOGUE   3
  Characters   3
    — *After Dinner*   3
    — *Definition*   5
    — *Enablers*   7
    — *Values*   8
    — *Love*   11
    — *Wealth*   13
    — *Truth*   14
    — *Lost*   16
    — *Compass*   17
    — *Knowledge*   19
    — *Philosophy*   22
    — *Wisdom*   23
    — *Worlds*   25
    — *Power, Authority*   27
    — *Signs*   30
    — *Objectification*   31
    — *Happiness*   33
    — *Good and Bad*   34
    — *Goodness*   36
    — *Conscience*   38
    — *The Good*   40
    — *Neutral*   42
    — *Tyranny*   44
    — *The Many*   47
    — *Punish, Reward*   49
    — *Courage and Hate*   50

— *Vision*   53
— *Tyranny 2*   55
— *Law*   56
— *Checks*   57
— *Inspiration*   59
— *The Tyrant in Me*   59
— *Death*   61
— *Words*   62
— *Hope*   63
— *Thought*   65
— *Color*   67
— *Happiness 2*   69
— *States of Mind*   71
— *Independence*   73
— *Trying*   75
— *Some Fun*   77
— *Implied*   79
— *Mercy*   81
— *Kites*   82
— *The Fight*   84
— *Fighting*   85
— *The Greatest Threat*   87
— *Love 2*   89
— *Potential*   90
— *Interest*   91
— *Knowledge 2*   92
— *Saying*   94
— *Night*   96
— *Funny*   98
— *Surrender*   99
— *Letting Go*   100
— *Wooing*   101
— *Pastime*   103
— *Madness*   106
— *Laughter*   107
— *Friendship*   109
— *Voids*   110
— *Alike*   112
— *Belief*   114
— *Fear*   115
— *Starving*   118
— *Flattery*   120
— *The Hidden*   121
— *Revenge*   123
— *Oaths*   124
— *Concern*   126

— *Sharing*   127
— *Depending*   129
— *Fame*   130
— *Fear 2*   132
— *Love 3*   134
— *The World*   136
— *Happiness 3*   137
— *Arrogance*   138
— *Difference*   140
— *A Jury*   141
— *Friends*   143
— *Arguments*   145
— *Teachers*   147
— *Doing*   148
— *Living*   150
— *Standing*   152
— *Nerve*   155
— *Friends 2*   156
— *Pigs and Horses*   157
— *Recovery*   159
— *Forgetting*   160
— *Souls*   161
— *Depths, Damage*   162
— *Persuasion*   163
— *Good*   164
— *Reason*   165
— *Benefits*   167
— *Heart*   168
— *Hard*   170
— *Fit 171*
— *Support*   172
— *Amoral*   173
— *Growth*   175
— *Useful*   177
— *Getting Out*   178
— *Beauty*   180
— *Sensitive*   182
— *Protection*   183
— *Enemies*   184
Philosophy 2   186
— *End*   187

INTRODUCTION

This book consists of a conversation between three characters: Builder, Director, and Senator. The conversation is about power. All three characters have power. All three have different notions of what power is.

Director is the constant character in all of my published books. He is a philosopher. In the course of the conversations in these books, light is shed on just what philosophy is.

So in reading this book one would do well to keep two questions in mind: What is power? And what is philosophy? Everything in the book aims to address these questions.

The emphasis is on power, however. The book is not entitled On Power and Philosophy. Why not?

Philosophy wants to know what something is—power in this case. Power is the object of philosophy. Philosophy is not the object of power. Power generally doesn't concern itself with philosophy—unless it wants to enlist its support, or philosophy becomes an irritant.

Director manages to engage the others in a lengthy conversation about power without being an irritant. That is his skill as a philosopher. That skill must not take center stage, however, as anyone who knows how to persuade will understand.

So center stage is left to power. Builder is proud of his power. He is the focus of the dialogue in several ways. Director focuses on him.

It's important to understand the interpersonal dynamics in play. Philosophy is concerned with these dynamics in a fundamental way. I'd go so far as to say that you cannot properly understand what philosophy is until you manage to understand what the various interpersonal dynamics mean when it comes to things such as knowledge and understanding—and power.

This is the main reason I write dialogues and not treatises. I feel there is a need to converse about topics of importance. And I have two small hopes. One, that these dialogues will stimulate thought about the topics discussed. Two, that readers will take them as a starting point and branch out beyond them into topics of importance to themselves—to be discussed with characters in their lives of importance to themselves.

Throughout my books of dialogues, the reader gets to assess how likely it is the characters will take these steps. The reasons both for and against are telling.

Nick Pappas

The Dialogue

Characters

Builder

Director

Senator

After Dinner

Senator: That was an excellent meal. Your chef outdid himself.

Builder: I'm glad you enjoyed it. He's great and I was lucky to find him. But not as lucky as I was when one of my managers found the man you see here. Without Director my last project would have died.

Senator: Then I'm even more glad to make your acquaintance tonight, Director.

Builder: Why, you want to try and steal him away?

Senator: I'd like to hear how he helped.

Director: I just saw a few things that needed to be done.

Builder: Yes, but you did them. That's more than I can say for most.

Senator: Yes, yes. I know. Our party doesn't do enough for you.

Builder: With all the millions I give, you'd think I'd have something more to show. But still, I'm a believer in what you do. Ha, ha. And what about you, Director? Are you a believer, too?

Director: I believe Senator's party is at the peak of its power.

Senator: But do you believe in our cause?

Builder: Cause? Power is the cause—the only cause. Believe in that. Now, Director, I hear you're a philosopher.

Director: Where did you hear that?

Builder: I have ears.

Director: Then those ears must know I'm a philosopher of the non-professional sort.

Senator: Why not professional?

Director: I'm not qualified.

Builder: I somehow doubt it.

Senator: I think Director doesn't want to taint philosophy with money.

Builder: Taint? Don't you know what money is? It's a vote of confidence. How is that a taint? But it's funny.

Senator: What's funny?

Builder: I have some confidence in you. And I'm a good judge of these things. But you only make a thousandth of what I earn!

Director: Are people that confident in you?

Builder: Yes. And my team had confidence in you. Do you know how I know?

Director: They asked you to pay for my help.

Builder: And you weren't cheap! So set Senator straight. Did that money interfere with your philosophy?

Director: No. I put it where it couldn't do any harm.

Senator: Where's that?

Director: I gave it to friends in need.

Senator: You kept nothing for yourself?

Director: No, I did keep something. And I keep it in my head.

Builder: Ha! What about you, Senator? Would you like some philosophy to keep in your head?

Senator: Sure, provided it serves as a moral compass. But what do you keep in your head, Builder?

Builder: My list of enemies. I remember them well.

Director: What wrong does it take to be your enemy?

Builder: Wrong? There are many wrongs. But my least favorite? The double-cross—deceit and betrayal.

Director: I can't believe you have many enemies from that.

Builder: Why not?

Director: Because to be deceived you have to believe. And who do you believe?

Builder: No one. Well, close to no one. I believe Senator here a little.

Director: Senator, would you ever try to double-cross this man?

Senator: Are you serious? Of course not.

Director: Because you're afraid of him?

Senator: No, not of him. I'm afraid of something else.

Director: What?

Senator: Losing my integrity.

Builder: Director, he's speaking strange words. Can you translate for me?

Director: He wants to feel good about himself.

Builder: As do we all.

Director: What makes you feel good about yourself, Builder?

Builder: Good? What makes anyone feel good? Power.

— Definition

Director: What is power?

Builder: The ability to get what you want.

Senator: But what gives you the ability?

Builder: Properly directed force.

Senator: Yes, but you don't always need force to get what you want.

Builder: True. Sometimes the mere threat of force is enough.

Director: Do you believe the world is the balance, and at times the imbalance, of forces?

Builder: Of course I do. And when it's imbalanced you strike.

Director: Strike it rich?

Builder: Yes. I think you could learn from me.

Senator: But do you want to be rich, Director?

Director: If it furthered philosophy? Sure.

Senator: So riches are only a means to an end for you.

Director: Only that, yes.

Senator: What's your end, Builder?

Builder: I'm in it for the thrill of the game.

Senator: Is that why you're in philosophy, Director?

Director: Philosophy certainly has its thrills. But in the end? No, that's not why I'm in it.

Senator: Then why?

Director: Would you believe me if I say I don't know?

Builder: How can you not know?

Director: Because philosophy came to me.

Senator: And you wouldn't turn it away?

Director: I fell in love.

Builder: With philosophy?

Director: Yes.

Builder: Was this in your imagination? A vision of Lady Philosophy, or some such thing?

Director: I don't even know how to begin to answer.

Builder: Then answer this. Does philosophy give you power?

Director: I give my power to philosophy.

Builder: Why?

Director: It seems like a good investment.

Builder: So what's your return?

Director: On investment? I get to come around.

Senator: Come around? Come around to what?

Builder: Oh, don't be such an ignoramus. He's talking about coming around to truth.

Director: Yes, but that's only part of it.

Builder: What more is there?

Director: Once you've come to truth, you have to decide what do with it.

Builder: Ah.

Senator: What?

Builder: Most people would say something like live the truth, share the truth, and so on. But Director? He says you have to decide. So what did you decide?

Director: That it's on a case by case basis.

Builder: And what are the cases? People?

Director: Yes, and what they need to hear when.

Builder: So what are you, some sort of doctor treating patients with truth? Then tell me, doctor—what ails me?

Director: You want more respect.

Senator: Now you're teasing.

Builder: But you know, he's right. I do want more respect. Others' confidence just isn't enough. You can have confidence in someone you don't much admire.

Senator: What's an example of that?

Builder: My enemies are confident my buildings will be great. They even invest in them. But they give me no respect.

Director: Do they admire your work?

Builder: Lust for profit takes the place of admiration in their hearts.

Senator: I know some people who admire your work. You should admire theirs.

Builder: What people?

Senator: Those who support you.

Builder: Support me? Who supports me?

Senator: We do. We who enable your work.

Builder: We? You and your political friends? Ha! I support you! And I give you all the respect—your kind deserves.

— Enablers

Director: Is there a time when your enablers don't enable?

Builder: Of course. When they get in the way. Do you know what they do?

Director: Tell us.

Builder: They make laws to snuff out sparks like me.

Senator: We only do that when you threaten to start a raging fire. We have to protect the people.

Builder: And who protects me? I'll tell you who. Director. Tell Senator what you did for me.

Director: I really didn't do much. I met with local officials and persuaded them to leave Builder's project alone.

Builder: He didn't do much! And yet it was invaluable. Can't you see the difference, Senator? Your party does little for me and calls it much. He does much and calls it little.

Senator: You don't appreciate how complex these things can be.

Builder: And you don't appreciate how simple they can be. Director does.

Senator: Then why not go into politics, Director?

Director: It's really not my thing.

Builder: And do you know why I think he says that?

Senator: Why?

Builder: Because he sees your example.

Senator: What's that supposed to mean?

Builder: I'll say it again. Power is the ability to get what you want. Your power, so to speak, is used up in getting things for others. You don't get what you want. You enact the wants of others.

Senator: How do you know that's not what I want?

Builder: You want what they want? No matter what they want? Oh, I feel sorry for you.

Director: But I don't.

Senator: Why not?

Director: Because you don't always do what they want.

Senator: That's true. They elected me because I sometimes know best.

Builder: The enabler enables himself.

Senator: No, I always put the voters first.

Builder: And how do you do that? I know. You bring them back pork.

Senator: It's not about that.

Builder: Isn't it? Director?

Director: Pork wins votes.

Senator: But other things do, too.

— Values

Builder: What other things?

Senator: Tell us. Why do you give money to the party? In hopes of pork?

Builder: That and certain adjustments to the law. Why? Should I have hoped for something else?

Senator: Don't you care about values?

Director: There's a significant block of value voters, Builder.

Builder: Bah.

Senator: That's all you can say?

Builder: What do these value voters want?

Senator: For one, they want honesty in government.

Builder: Good luck with that.

Director: Is an honest politician impossible?

Builder: Of course

Senator: Why?

Builder: Everyone wants something from you. The truth is, you can do very little. But your opponent promises everything. So you lie to keep up. You make false promises. That's how I think it starts. And it snowballs from there.

Director: Senator?

Senator: Yes, but people really do want honesty. They're not stupid. They know I can't get everything done. They want me to take a stand on certain things. And while they'd rather we win, they're happy to know we're fighting the fight.

Builder: I'm hung up on just one thing. 'They're not stupid.' I'm not so sure about that. While I believe some of your voters are very smart, I know that can't be the rule. So how do you deal with the dumb?

Senator: I keep things very simple for them.

Builder: But that's a lie, too. You yourself just said political things are complex.

Senator: I said they can be complex.

Builder: And when they are?

Senator: I do the best I can.

Builder: It takes power to keep things simple, you know.

Senator: I know.

Builder: It takes a great amount of force.

Senator: No, it takes the power of persuasion.

Builder: Persuasion is merely less obvious force.

Senator: That's not true. Persuasion and force are two completely different things.

Builder: How so?

Senator: Would you rather be persuaded or forced?

Builder: I'd rather do the persuading or forcing myself.

Senator: I can understand that concerning force. But you never want to be persuaded?

Builder: Why would I? Give me an example.

Senator: Say you're working late, as you always do, and I drop by and persuade you to take a break and have dinner with me.

Builder: That would never happen. But it might with you.

Senator: What do you mean?

Builder: You might be working hard when I drop by. But I persuade you to come to dinner with me.

Senator: Why am I persuaded but not you?

Builder: Two reasons. One, you know I'm there because I want to talk business. Two, you're worried I might take offense if you refuse. And who knows what that offense might bring?

Director: But you don't worry when you refuse.

Builder: Of course I don't. And that says much about where Senator and I stand in life.

Director: It says something about your values, too.

Builder: How so?

Director: Senator, let me hazard a guess. You value your work. But you also value taking a break. You value leisure. So if you have a chance to get away, and it won't harm your work, you take it.

Senator: True.

Director: And you, Builder, you value—love—your work. So you never want a break. You really don't value leisure. Or have I got it wrong?

Builder: No, you're absolutely right. I love what I do. I'll have time for leisure when I'm dead. And I want to work with others who feel that way, too.

Senator: No one loves their work quite like you.

Builder: Yes, but let me tell you a thing I learned about Director, here. He slept in the office many nights until the project was secure.

Director: But that wasn't out of love.

Senator: What was it out of?

Director: Maybe it was fear. Fear that I'd fail.

Builder: But that's the best value of all! That's what drives me.

Senator: I thought love drove you.

Builder: Love, fear—they go together. You fear you'll lose what you love.

— Love

Director: What about power and fear? Is it the same sort of thing?

Builder: Yes, of course. You fear you'll lose your power.

Director: Because you love power.

Builder: We all love power.

Director: What does it take to love power the right way?

Builder: I don't understand.

Director: I mean, does it take knowledge? Do you have to know how to love?

Builder: Oh, I see. You do need to know how to love. And since knowledge is power, we can say you need power in order to love power as you should.

Director: Power is truly a wonderful thing.

Builder: Ha, ha. Yes, Director, it is.

Director: But tell us something, Builder. When you have power like yours, is it better to be loved or feared?

Builder: If you have to pick one it ought to be fear. There's more power there. But it's best to let fear lead to love. Then you have both.

Senator: No one loves what they fear.

Builder: Really? You haven't seen enough of life.

Senator: I've seen enough to know I want to be loved without fear.

Builder: We'll see who gets further in the end.

Director: What does it mean to get further?

Builder: To have more power.

Senator: Then you'd better focus on love, not fear.

Builder: Why?

Senator: Love has more power.

Builder: Tell me how so.

Senator: Love can overcome fear. But fear can't overcome love.

Builder: You must not know many cowards.

Senator: Cowards don't love. It takes courage to love. Love risks all.

Builder: Certain gamblers risk all. Are they courageous?

Senator: If you can't tell the difference between gambling and love, I can't help you here.

Builder: Okay, Senator. But let's be plain. The love that brings you power is the love from another. Their love gives you power over them.

Senator: No, that's not what I mean. Your own love gives you power.

Builder: I don't think we'll ever agree on this.

Director: Builder, are you saying if someone gives you love, you'd take advantage of them?

Builder: Yes, but not in the way you might imagine.

Senator: I, on the other hand, would be a great support.

Builder: How would you be a support?

Senator: By being honest with them.

Builder: And what does honesty involve?

Senator: Not manipulating them.

Builder: But it's okay to manipulate others outside the circle of love?

Senator: No, I'm not saying that.

Director: Would you let your lovers manipulate you?

Senator: Not if I could help it. But why are you asking? Why speak of lovers with me?

Builder: Ha, ha. He noticed your handsome looks.

Senator: I'm more stately than handsome.

Builder: The two are the same, to some. But here's the real reason why you have lovers. You have a degree of power.

Senator: And you think we should be loved for our power?

Builder: It's not a matter of 'should'.

Senator: But what does that get us? And don't say advantage.

Builder: You tell me.

Senator: Director, what do you think?

Director: I can only speak to love in general. And what does it get us? At best? Friendship.

Builder: At best, yes. Which is to say not always. Which can mean very rarely indeed. But that's fine, because friendship can be a distraction.

Senator: From what?

Builder: Power. What else?

— Wealth

Director: Builder, when you exercise power, what's your aim?

Builder: I'll tell you one aim. Building wealth where there was none.

Director: Are wealth and love somehow incompatible? Or can we use love to build wealth?

Senator: Director, why are you even asking that?

Director: Because I want to know.

Senator: Yes, but the answer should be obvious.

Director: Then tell us what it is.

Senator: We can't take advantage of love.

Builder: Advantage? What if our lover wants to help us build wealth?

Senator: That's not the purpose of love.

Builder: What is the purpose of love?

Senator: Love itself.

Builder: Then let's build monuments of wealth to love.

Senator: Love is the only monument to love.

Builder: Even when love only goes one way?

Senator: True love never goes one way.

Builder: And you say that to a man with a face as ugly as mine.

Director: It's true. Many would say you have an ugly face. But that never stopped love.

Builder: What would they love me for?

Director: They'd love you for you.

Builder: Ha, ha. You mean they'd love me for my wealth.

Director: Doesn't your wealth derive from you?

Builder: What, from my courage and strength? But what about Senator's kind of courage and strength?

Director: His kind? That wins him love, too. Or don't you agree?

Builder: No, Senator deserves his share of love. But if my courage and strength, my virtue, brings wealth—what does his bring?

Senator: Justice.

Builder: What a shame.

Senator: A shame?

Builder: Your virtue could bring you money.

Senator: And that's what you think is best?

Builder: I haven't said what I think is best. But, unlike you, I'm not one to look down my nose at wealth.

Senator: Why not?

Builder: Because that's where the action is.

— Truth

Senator: I prefer the things that can't be bought.

Builder: What can't be bought?

Senator: Truth.

Builder: Most truth is overpriced. That's why it seems it can't be bought.

Director: Why is it overpriced?

Builder: People hold it for ransom.

Director: Even as others starve for truth?

Builder: Especially then.

Senator: So they price gouge truth.

Builder: Yes, they do.

Director: But you don't?

Builder: I'd give away truth for free if I could.

Director: Why can't you?

Builder: I have to make a living.

Senator: You take advantage of those who starve.

Builder: Oh, take it easy, Senator. For a small price I give them the food they need.

Director: How much food do they need?

Builder: Most of them? Not much. But you and me? We're never full.

Senator: And what about me?

Builder: You? You're so full of truth, or something like that, you can't compare.

Senator: Something like that?

Builder: Oh, you know. Empty platitudes that sound good to a crowd.

Senator: Platitudes don't sound good to the crowds that gather for me.

Director: What sounds good to them?

Senator: Truth!

Builder: Yes, but there's truth—and then there's truth.

Director: For instance, on the one hand, it's true the sky is blue on a sunny day?

Builder: Ha, ha. Yes, you know exactly what I mean.

Director: And it's true that when a tornado comes....

Builder: No need to complete the thought. But that's why we need power. That's why we need force.

Senator: Because you can force the tornado away?

Builder: You know I don't think that. But when it comes time to rebuild? Who would you rather have? Someone weak, or someone who commands great force?

Director: Someone who commands the force, I think. But I wonder about that.

Builder: Oh?

Director: Does it take great force to direct great force? Or can you be relatively weak and accomplish that same end?

Builder: Ask Senator. He's relatively weak and thinks he commands great force.

Senator: I am relatively weak. But I'm strong in truth.

Builder: You're strong in campaign funds.

Senator: People like to give to the cause.

Builder: Let me guess. The cause of truth.

Senator: Yes. And my service to that cause is what you love about me.

Builder: I love you for so many reasons. Why limit it to truth?

Senator: But you must admit. You do love truth—in others.

Builder: Why do you think that is?

Senator: Because you think the truthful are simpletons, easily manipulated.

Builder: Director, do you hear what this man is saying?

Director: I do. And I can't say I'm pleased if it's true.

Builder: What would please you?

Director: For you to say the truthful are like rocks that can't be moved.

Builder: Rocks, yes—in the head.

— Lost

Senator: Rocks aside, once you start manipulating it's very hard to stop. It's like trying to find your way out of a maze.

Director: What does it take to get out?

Senator: Memory of where you've been.

Builder: You don't need to bother with that.

Director: Why not?

Builder: If you have enough power, you just knock down the walls. But not all with power want to leave.

Director: Do you?

Builder: No. I like to watch others panic when they're lost. They come to me, you know.

Director: In your corner? Why?

Builder: Because power attracts.

Senator: Money attracts.

Builder: Money is the distillate of power. So, yes, money attracts.

Director: But is money really that, the distillate of power?

Builder: What else would it be?

Director: I don't know.

Builder: I'm starting to think you're not as sharp as I thought.

Director: I might not be sharp, but I know this. Sometimes money and power have nothing to do with one another.

Builder: Tell me when.

Director: When, for instance, someone wins the lottery. Do you think that person has power?

Builder: No, almost never. Not real power. So you have a point. But your exception proves the rule. What counts is earning your wealth.

Director: Why?

Builder: Because otherwise you're just lost in the cash.

Director: What makes for power when you earn your wealth?

Builder: Knowledge.

Senator: Knowledge of how to use it?

Builder: Of course.

Director: How should wealth be used?

Builder: To good effect.

Director: What does that mean?

Builder: To grow more wealth.

Director: The purpose of wealth is wealth?

Builder: Look, when you play soccer, what's the purpose of a goal?

Director: You score in order to win.

Builder: Well, that's the purpose of wealth. Whoever has the most wins.

— Compass

Director: And that provides a compass? When in doubt, go to where the money is?

Builder: That's what everyone does—or would like to do.

Senator: Not all of us. But is that what you'd teach your children?

Builder: If I had any children? Sure, I'd teach them this. They'd learn from me that money is ninety-nine percent of life.

Senator: And what's the remaining one percent?

Builder: Sleep.

Senator: What an empty life.

Builder: Senator, don't be jealous. How do you spend ninety-nine percent of your time?

Senator: In serving others.

Builder: And what do you get from that?

Senator: Satisfaction. That's my compass. I go to where the satisfaction is.

Director: And that's often in passing good legislation?

Senator: Yes, of course.

Director: What makes legislation good?

Senator: It's good for the voters.

Builder: And what's good for the voters? I'll tell you. Tax cuts and jobs.

Director: Things that give them more money.

Builder: Yes. Senator, do you disagree?

Senator: More money for the common voter is good.

Builder: The common voter. You mean the not-so-rich.

Senator: I do.

Builder: Do you look down on them?

Senator: What? Of course not.

Builder: But they're concerned with money for themselves—unlike you, with your more noble view.

Senator: And what's your view?

Builder: Hardly noble. And all for myself.

Senator: I think you're misguided.

Builder: I should be concerned with satisfaction, like you? But money satisfies, my friend. It's a reflection of my power.

Senator: And what happens when you follow power as your inner compass?

Builder: Easier to say what happens when you don't. Just look at you. You say your compass is satisfaction. Well, who doesn't want that? But there's satisfaction, and then there's satisfaction. Should I give an example?

Senator: Please.

Builder: You might go to a very expensive restaurant and drink very rare wine and eat a very large meal. Would you be satisfied?

Senator: Well....

Builder: Oh, don't be a prude. You'd be satisfied. But my point is this. What if you do this every single day, for every meal? You'd be fat and broke. Does your compass point true?

Senator: Of course not.

Builder: Yes. But if I spend every single day using my power to gain more money, for the sake of more power, I'm never fat and broke.

Senator: Nor are you satisfied. You always want more.

Builder: True, but I have my satisfactions along the way.

Senator: But you need to know when enough is enough.

Builder: Director, what do you think?

Director: I'm with Senator.

Senator: You see? Director knows.

Builder: Why do you side with him?

Director: Because he puts satisfaction together with knowledge. You have to know, know when enough is enough—or you ruin your satisfaction. No?

Builder: No. For some things there's never enough.

Senator: Moderation in all things, my friend.

Builder: Moderation even in knowledge? Or should we always know more?

Senator: I know what you're playing at. Knowledge is power. So if we can never have enough knowledge, we can never have enough power.

Builder: And it's true. What do you say, Director? Still on the wrong side?

Director: I'm hung up on the translation.

Builder: The translation?

Director: Of knowledge into power.

Builder: Why are you hung up on that?

Director: Because I can't help but feel that in it—something essential is lost.

Knowledge

Builder: But what's lost? Here's an example. If I know your weaknesses, I can exploit them. That's knowledge and power, and nothing is lost.

Senator: But you might not know why he has the weaknesses he has. Your knowledge is incomplete.

Builder: Power doesn't need complete knowledge.

Senator: And that's Director's point.

Builder: Was that your point, Director? Director?

Director: Sorry, I was caught up in thought.

Builder: About what?

Director: The other way.

Builder: What other way?

Director: The translation of power into knowledge. I was wondering if something is lost there, too.

Senator: What can we translate from power?

Director: What power does.

Senator: What's an example?

Builder: I'll give you an example. Making money. That's an exercise of power.

Senator: And when the powerful try to translate their actions into words, into knowledge for others—what happens then?

Builder: You assume it's the powerful who do the translating.

Senator: Who else would?

Builder: Witnesses to their actions.

Director: Who would do the better job?

Builder: Hold on. We're not yet done with the assumptions.

Senator: What else are we assuming?

Builder: That the translation is into words.

Director: Can you say more?

Builder: Someone can witness power and come to know, with nothing written or said.

Director: And nothing is lost?

Builder: Something is certainly lost. And the one who wants to know has to supply this something on their own.

Director: Without the something there is no knowledge from power?

Builder: It's worse than that. People without the something think they have knowledge of power. And they couldn't be more wrong.

Director: What is the something, Builder?

Builder: Ha! That's just what can't be said.

Senator: I know what it is. It's love.

Builder: What kind of love?

Senator: Love of the exercise of power.

Builder: That's not too far from right.

Director: Can you learn to love the exercise of power?

Builder: If you have to learn.... But I'll tell you what you have to learn. You have to learn to stop stopping yourself from loving the exercise of power.

Senator: Did you have to stop stopping yourself from loving the making of money?

Builder: I did. And then I was free. Have you ever stopped stopping?

Senator: I love helping the voters. I never stopped myself here. And maybe that's because I don't need any money for this.

Builder: Do you think that puts you on the moral high ground? But you're right, you don't need any money—your money, at least.

Senator: You're talking about taxes.

Builder: What else? You collect more of them than I like to think. What does it say about you when you rely on others' money?

Senator: All money was once someone else's money.

Builder: How clever to say. Does this money satisfy you?

Senator: Only when it's put to good use.

Builder: Why can't the citizens put their money to good use themselves? Why can't they mind their own affairs?

Senator: Some things require collective action.

Builder: And you're a leader of the collective.

Director: You're not satisfied with his work?

Builder: No I'm not satisfied.

Senator: Do you think you could do better yourself?

Builder: At leading a collective? Of course not. But I'll tell you this. I contribute more than my fair share.

Senator: Oh, you're only doing your part. You should feel satisfied with that.

Builder: I'd feel satisfied if I got my money back.

Director: Maybe you can through writing a book.

Builder: Ha, ha. And what do you think I'd call it?

Director: 'More than Fair: Serving the People'.

Builder: And if Senator wrote a book?

Director: 'My Passion is You'.

Builder: That sounds a little creepy, you know. But somehow very appropriate!

Director: Tell us, Senator. Does it make sense to have a passion for someone you don't know?

Senator: No, knowledge is key. That's why my number one job is to know the people.

Director: Knowledge comes first. Do you hear that, Builder?

Builder: Yes, so politics and philosophy have something in common. Wonderful. But I need to know people—and know them well—for what I do. Do I have something in common with you?

Director: I think you do. But then the question is what we do with our knowledge. You make money. Senator gets votes. But I....

Builder: Are you at a loss?

Director: I'm afraid what I'll say won't sound like much, especially when compared with things such as money and votes.

Builder: Then why not try for money? Or even votes, if you're so inclined?

Director: But that's the thing. I'm inclined toward neither, though I do need money and sometimes need to carry a vote.

Senator: So tell us what you do with your knowledge.

Builder: I know what he does.

Director: You do?

Builder: Of course. You make a philosophy of it.

— Philosophy

Senator: Is that what you do?

Director: Not quite.

Builder: Why not?

Director: I think you misunderstand what philosophy is.

Builder: Oh? What is it?

Director: It has to do with beliefs.

Builder: Say more.

Director: Philosophy attempts to turn belief into knowledge.

Builder: That's all philosophy does?

Director: No, there's more to it than that. But for our purposes tonight, I think we should start with this.

Builder: So if I believe a business plan is good, philosophy will try to make it so I know it's good?

Director: Or bad.

Senator: But philosophy doesn't care about business plans and such.

Builder: Director cared about them when he worked for me.

Senator: Then what is philosophy? "Nothing other" than good advice?

Director: It's not "nothing other," but yes, we can say it's good advice.

Senator: But that cheapens philosophy.

Builder: What's cheap about good advice? I'd say it's priceless.

Senator: But advice about what, precisely? Business matters? That's philosophy's concern?

Builder: The word 'business' covers a lot of ground.

Director: Yes, including advice about others.

Senator: People? Then you should come and work for me! I could use a good judge of character on my staff. But tell us the rest.

Director: The rest of philosophy?

Senator: Yes. You said it attempts to turn belief into knowledge. How?

Director: You're going to laugh. But I'll say it anyway. Philosophy helps turn belief into knowledge—by encouraging people to know when they merely believe.

Senator: And that says... nothing!

Builder: Oh, he's just teasing. But I know what he suggests.

Senator: Then tell us.

Builder: I believe I'm a successful person. But philosophy wants me to know it, know what I merely believe. How can I come to know?

Senator: How?

Builder: The philosopher defines success in my terms.

Senator: Director, is that what you do?

Director: We define success together. And then I tell my friend the truth.

Builder: Watch out, Senator. The truth might be you're a failure! But this is comical.

Director: Why?

Builder: Because I've learned enough of our language to know what the word philosophy means.

Senator: What does it mean?

Builder: It's the love of wisdom.

Director: And that's comical?

Builder: It is—because you're spending your time with us.

— Wisdom

Senator: I'd say between the three of us there's one wise man.

Builder: It depends what you mean by wisdom.

Director: What do you mean by wisdom?

Builder: Me? Knowing what to do with the characters you meet.

Director: And you know what to do?

Builder: I do.

Director: So you were just teasing us now. You know you're wise. And there's nothing funny in a philosopher spending time with you.

Builder: It's true. I'm wise. My success is proof. And there's nothing funny in that.

Director: Then maybe you can help me with something I've often wondered. What do the wise do with the wise?

Builder: For the most part? They keep their distance.

Director: Why?

Builder: Because they find it difficult to be around those who are wise to their ways.

Senator: So if you spend lots of time with the wise, it means you're unwise?

Director: Or something in-between.

Builder: In-between, yes. But tell us, Director. What do the wise do with the unwise?

Director: I think you should say.

Builder: Why, because I'm wise? Ha, ha. Alright. The wise manipulate the unwise.

Senator: No, that's not at all what they do.

Builder: What do they do?

Senator: They deal with others in a constructive way. My grandmother did this. She didn't manipulate the less-than-wise. She dealt with them in a way that strengthened their belief in themselves.

Builder: Were you very young when she was doing this?

Senator: Well, yes.

Builder: Then how would you know that's what it was? I, on the other hand, was lucky. My grandfather was wise. And he was powerful in mind until a very old age. So I learned the true ways of wisdom from him from youth on up.

Director: You learned to manipulate others.

Builder: Yes.

Senator: And you think that's good?

Builder: It is good.

Senator: How so?

Builder: Many people lack purpose, guidance in their lives. Manipulation can help.

Senator: Can help the manipulator.

Builder: If the manipulator is wise, it can help both.

Senator: Director?

Director: I'd need to spend time with the wise ones in question to see if this is true.

Senator: But it's false on its face!

Builder: Senator, I think you just need another name for manipulation, to make you feel at ease.

Senator: What name?

Builder: Persuasion.

Senator: No, no, no. Persuasion is good. Manipulation is bad.

Builder: Why is it bad?

Senator: Because when you manipulate someone, you go against their interests.

Builder: And persuasion aligns with interest?

Senator: Of course it does. So the truly wise persuade the unwise.

Director: I can go along with that. Builder?

Builder: Persuade, manipulate—they're the same to me. But who really knows another's interests?

Senator: The wise.

Builder: How do they know?

Senator: They know the world.

Builder: And so they know everyone's proper place in that world?

Senator: Well, that raises a question. You say 'that world'. Is there more than one world?

Builder: Of course there is. And each wise one rules their own.

— Worlds

Senator: Then I have no doubt you think you're wise, because you pride yourself on ruling your world.

Builder: That doesn't necessarily follow. But I do rule my world. Ask anyone in it.

Senator: Well, I rule no world at all. I guess I can't be wise.

Director: What if you could be wise without ruling a thing?

Builder: Then what's the point of wisdom? You can't separate wisdom from rule.

Senator: But what do we mean by rule? You can rule others, or you can rule yourself. Director seems wise in the latter.

Builder: It's all but impossible to be wise only in that sense.

Senator: Why?

Builder: Because people will try to interfere.

Director: You mean they'll barge into my world.

Builder: You know they will. They'll try to dominate you.

Senator: But clearly they're in the wrong.

Builder: Of course they're in the wrong. When someone rules their own life, and only their life, leave them alone. That's my principle. That's my code.

Director: Tell us, Builder, just to be sure. Is each self-ruled life a world?

Builder: Yes.

Director: Do we all have the right to rule our own world?

Builder: We have to earn that right.

Director: How did I earn my right?

Builder: If you have? Through practicing self-defense.

Director: Can everyone learn self-defense?

Builder: Enough to secure their own world? In theory, yes. But that kind of defense is hard.

Director: Even so, would you say it's irresponsible not to learn it?

Builder: Yes, and the irresponsible have no right. But what do you say, Senator? You trade in irresponsibility.

Senator: Because I defend those who can't defend themselves?

Builder: Because you rule those without the right to rule themselves.

Senator: You seem to have forgotten the distinction between public and private. I deal with the public, and leave the private alone.

Director: Which is more important? The public or the private?

Senator: They're equally important.

Builder: So your laws rule half a person's life? Then no one can completely rule their life on their own?

Senator: There has to be a place for community.

Builder: Director, would you live outside your community in order to rule your whole life?

Director: Living outside a community is all but impossible, my friend. And who says it's good?

Builder: Then what would you do?

Director: Live within and without at once.

Senator: What do you mean?

Director: My body lives within. My mind, in part, without. Unless...

Builder: Unless what?

Director: ...Senator and his friends come to legislate thought.

— Power, Authority

Senator: What would be the point? We'd lose our freedom.

Builder: We're stronger when we all think and believe as one.

Senator: That's fascist, Builder.

Builder: Oh, I'm as opposed to it as you are.

Director: You believe in the value of diversity?

Builder: Yes, so long as everyone agrees on some basic things.

Senator: You mean, so long as everyone supports the basic power structure.

Builder: Power structures exist for good reason—as you should full well know.

Director: What reason?

Builder: They're the bulwark against anarchy.

Director: How so?

Builder: Power, and in this case I mean the power that comes from property, is an organizing principle. Without that organization anything goes.

Director: Anything?

Builder: Crime, Director.

Director: Theft of property, namely.

Builder: Yes, of course. But other things follow from that. Are you opposed to these things, Senator?

Senator: Of course I am.

Builder: And yet you favor legal theft.

Senator: Taxes, you mean.

Builder: Yes. Too much taxation can wreck the structure, you know.

Director: But isn't the structure stronger than that?

Builder: How so?

Director: Think about homes, and schools, and so on. They all lend support.

Builder: And the wrong laws can undermine them, too. I would know. I have much in common with parents, teachers, and so on.

Senator: What could you possibly have in common with them?

Builder: They have power over their charges—and I have power over mine.

Senator: Who? The people you hire?

Builder: Yes. I have authority over them.

Senator: And what about my authority?

Builder: Your authority? Yours is more complex. You have some sort of authority over us. But we, the voters, have authority over you.

Senator: Some sort of authority? I have the authority of making law.

Builder: Yes, but the laws have the real authority, not you. But what about you, Director? What authority have you got?

Director: I had authority when I spoke in your name.

Senator: Borrowed authority.

Director: True. Beyond that? I have none.

Builder: But let's forget about authority. What power have you got?

Director: Power over myself?

Builder: He puts it as a question! Would you trade that power away?

Director: I don't think I would.

Senator: Of course you wouldn't. Without that power we're nothing.

Director: So if the highest executives in the land have no power over themselves, they're nothing?

Senator: Are you surprised that's what I think?

Director: No. But how can we tell if someone has this power?

Senator: The first thing we notice is that they're not interested in power over others. They might have that power through the hand of fate. But it's not something they long for or lust over.

Director: But they long for power within?

Senator: With their whole heart, yes.

Director: Why wouldn't everyone long for that?

Builder: That's a good question. Do you, Senator?

Senator: I do. Director?

Director: Nothing is more important.

Builder: Yes, and this all sounds fine. But here's a problem. I have power over myself, and yet I love to rule others. What does that make me?

Senator: A would-be tyrant.

Builder: But seriously. Director, what does that make me in your eyes?

Director: Someone who has to be careful.

Builder: About what?

Director: Finding your level.

Builder: You mean, I need more power.

Director: Yes.

Senator: What? This is ridiculous! Don't you know what happens if he keeps on seeking more and more power?

Builder: Oh, don't be a fool. The point is that I need more power within, in order to match the power without.

Senator: Then let's be more clear about what we mean when we say power within.

Builder: It means I don't listen to anyone else.

Director: It means you listen carefully to others.

Builder: Why would it mean that?

Director: Because you can't rule yourself unless you have the best ideas.

Builder: But what if I already have the best ideas?

Director: You need to keep proving that to yourself. And you prove it by weighing what you think against what others think.

Senator: And if he closes his mind and refuses to hear?

Director: Things get bad.

Senator: For us or for him?

Director: Likely both. And that's why we look for warning signs. Before it's too late.

— Signs

Senator: So what are the signs?

Director: They have to do with pleasure.

Builder: I'd love to hear this.

Director: There are two sorts of pleasure in question here. One that has to do with ideas, and one that has to do with rule.

Builder: Say more.

Director: If you take more pleasure in rule than ideas, you're in trouble.

Builder: What kind of trouble?

Senator: Oh, you know what kind. He's saying it's a bad sign, and that taking more pleasure in ideas is good.

Builder: So what if you take pleasure in rule, but take greater pleasure in ideas about rule? What kind of sign is that?

Director: It depends. So tell us. Is it a pleasure to rule?

Builder: Rule is hard.

Director: It's sometimes far from pleasant?

Builder: If it's done well? Yes.

Director: Then who simply takes pleasure in rule?

Builder: Those who won't rule for long.

Director: But those who rule well, the ones for whom it's hard—they can take pleasure in ideas about rule, maybe enough so to compensate them for their trouble?

Builder: It's possible.

Senator: It's possible? Why else would you rule? You need something to sustain you. So what sustains you?

Builder: You mean, what idea?

Senator: Yes.

Builder: That's a very personal thing.

Senator: It's fine if you'd rather not say. But I'll tell you what sustains me. The idea of the greater good.

Builder: The greater good? What kind of idea is that? I'll tell you what 'greater good' means to most. Their own interests writ large. So tell me—are the laws in your interest?

Senator: Good laws are in the interest of all.

Builder: So it's a bad sign when they work for some but not others.

Senator: Of course. I'm sure Director agrees.

Director: Yes, but I'd like to know what Builder means by 'others'.

Senator: What do you mean?

Director: Does he mean, for instance, when he's filling out a form, and there are ten categories to choose from in describing himself, and none of them fits—he marks 'other', and leaves it at that?

Senator: I don't think that's what he had in mind,

Builder: But I always have this in mind. That's my life story. Other. And the laws don't work for me—except when I make them.

Director: What does it mean for a law to work for you?

Senator: To work for means to protect.

Builder: And you think the laws can protect us all? Historically, is that true?

Senator: Of course it's not true, not absolutely.

Builder: And you didn't even ask who is 'us all'.

Senator: Who is 'us all'?

Builder: The ones chosen by the powers that be. The powers define 'us'—and then they make laws.

Director: Is it a good sign when 'us' is as broad as can be?

Senator: Of course it is.

Builder: I disagree.

Senator: Why? You claim to be other. Don't you want to be included?

Builder: Yes, but there are people I don't want as part of my us.

Senator: Well, we all have people we don't like.

Builder: But I mean something more. I don't want the people I use included with me.

Senator: We all use each other, loosely speaking, every day.

Builder: I'm talking about a particular kind of use. The kind where the people in question are nothing more—than objects to me.

— Objectification

Director: Senator, what's the problem with objectification?

Senator: It takes away a person's humanity.

Director: How does it happen?

Senator: You should ask Builder.

Builder: It happens through having no care for the other, except as means.

Director: Yes, but I wonder if there's something more. If you don't know someone, anyone, for what they are, which is to say who they are—do you objectify them in a way?

Builder: You take them for other than they are? Sure, that might objectify them. To you they're not what they are. They're objects in your mind.

Senator: So what does that mean? If you know them for who they are, you can't objectify them?

Builder: Of course you can objectify those you know. You know they're good for use as means.

Senator: But do you know them? I mean, really?

Builder: The better you know them the better their use.

Senator: But what if you know they don't want to be used?

Builder: Then you forget about that. You close your mind.

Senator: I would never look at anyone as an object.

Builder: Do you know all those you represent? I mean, really know them—know each for who they are?

Senator: If I don't, they're objects to me?

Builder: Aren't they?

Senator: Not at all. I humanize them as much as I can. You, on the other hand.... That's all the difference here. I wouldn't be surprised if you tried to objectify Director!

Builder: As what? Some problem solving machine?

Senator: Why not?

Director: Builder, if you saw me only as that, your mind would be closed?

Builder: Yes.

Director: Your mind would have to be open to know me for what I am?

Builder: Of course.

Director: Do you know me for what I am?

Builder: I do. But let me tell you something. You're a human, but you're also a problem solving machine. Two things at once. And that's what's hard, that's the real power here. Being able to see both at once.

Director: Yes, but I wonder.

Builder: What do you wonder?

Director: I'm afraid this will sound impious or worse.

Builder: All the more reason to say it.

Director: Maybe, in the way of our world today, we know people first as machines—before we know them as human beings.

Builder: Because we're what we do? Demolition workers, for instance, demolish. So they are, first and foremost, demolition machines? And only through knowing them as that do we have access to their humanity?

Director: What do you think?

Builder: It's true.

— Happiness

Senator: This is ridiculous. First and foremost, we need to know people as human beings. It doesn't matter what they do.

Builder: It doesn't matter? What kind of human being are you when you hate what you do? I'll answer. You're a miserable human being. You can't deny that.

Director: And when you love what you do?

Builder: You're happy. And I'll tell you this. Knowledge of happiness or unhappiness gives you power.

Senator: How?

Builder: If you know someone is unhappy, you can manipulate them by promising better work, a better life.

Director: And if you know they're happy?

Builder: You can threaten to take away what they love.

Senator: Leave it to you to think of these things.

Builder: But you know I'm right. Power over happiness is the greatest power of all.

Senator: Yes, but we ourselves have that power, not others.

Builder: Don't be so sure.

Director: Builder, tell us. What's the greater power? Making someone happy or unhappy?

Builder: It's relatively easy to make someone unhappy. Making happy is harder.

Director: Because it takes a constant effort?

Builder: No, you just give them what they want and leave them alone.

Senator: Assuming it's in your power to give.

Builder: That's what's hard.

Senator: People sometimes think they know what they want, but don't.

Builder: True. And sometimes they don't know what to think.

Director: And sometimes they know what they want but can't put it in words.

Senator: People often rely on luck.

Director: If you discover happiness by chance, can it last?

Builder: It's possible.

Senator: You need the right frame of mind. It's a matter of belief.

Director: Belief in what?

Senator: The power of positive things.

— Good and Bad

Builder: You really think positive things have the power to make happiness last?

Senator: I do.

Builder: But why do you have to believe in this power? Why can't you know it for a fact? And what about negative things?

Senator: What about them?

Builder: They have a power of their own, don't they?

Senator: I suppose.

Builder: Of course they do! And do you know what? We feel them more than the positive.

Director: They have more power?

Builder: That's right.

Senator: Just what I'd expect from you.

Director: So if someone loves power, they should align with the negative? Do you align with the negative, Builder?

Builder: I do. I don't much rely on the positive.

Director: Would you say the negative is bad?

Builder: Bad? I don't know what that word means.

Director: What about good? Is the positive good?

Builder: If I don't know bad, how can I know good?

Director: Then tell us this. Is it possible for something to be neither bad nor good?

Builder: Ah. Now you're asking something interesting. Yes, it's possible. And that's what I am.

Director: But do people see it that way?

Builder: No. They like to hang a sign on things and call them good or bad.

Director: And when they do, you think of their bad as 'bad' and their good as 'good'?

Builder: You understand this well.

Director: If asked by someone who doesn't know you, would you say you're aligned with the good?

Builder: I certainly would.

Director: Why?

Builder: Because it gives me an advantage with them.

Director: You're willing to employ deceit.

Builder: If the person is truly 'good' you have to.

Director: Why?

Builder: Because it's almost certain they'll be dense.

Director: Dense?

Builder: Thick in the head.

Director: You mean they don't think very well.

Builder: Right.

Senator: Why don't you help them think?

Builder: Oh, I've tried. But there's no getting through.

Senator: Still, you should side with them.

Builder: Why?

Senator: Because the good are the greatest power on Earth.

Builder: I know that's what you think. But tell me why it's so.

Senator: Because the good never give up or give in.

Builder: And you think the bad do?

Senator: The bad have no faith to support them. And so they can't struggle or resist for long.

Director: This faith, Senator, is it in the power of truth?

Senator: It absolutely is.

Builder: You think truth always prevails?

Senator: In the long run? Yes.

Builder: Well, you're more of a fool than I thought. Do you believe all history is truth?

Senator: No, of course not.

Builder: Do you believe all that is was meant to be?

Senator: It's hard to say.

Builder: I don't think it's hard. And the answer is no, not all that is was meant to be.

Director: How so, Builder?

Builder: There's a difference between intent and effect.

Director: And the intent is the meant-to-be?

Builder: Yes. You've heard of unintended consequences?

Director: I have.

Builder: Do you believe they happen?

Director: I know they do.

Builder: Who has more of them?

Director: The good or the bad? I don't know.

Senator: What? Why don't you know? It's obviously the bad.

Builder: Why?

Senator: Because the bad lie. And truth is always more likely—to get you what you want.

— Goodness

Builder: And the good are truthful?

Senator: Of course they are.

Builder: Well, my friend, I take a more sophisticated view. The good aren't always true. And when they're not, that's often when they get what they want.

Director: So you don't believe truth has a power, a power that helps you get what you want?

Builder: There's not much power in truth alone. That's an old myth. We can use truth, yes. But to believe in it blindly? Ha.

Senator: But the power of truth in the hands of the good is almost always much.

Builder: The hands of the 'good' or the good?

Director: You tell us.

Builder: Let's talk about the truly good. The notion that they almost always have much power goes against the entire experience of the world.

Director: Does it?

Builder: Why would you doubt?

Director: Because the good coordinate their strengths.

Builder: And the less than good don't?

Director: Not nearly as much.

Builder: So coordinated strengths prevail over uncoordinated strengths? Give us an example.

Director: Okay. Here's one. I once watched a game of lacrosse. One team, the home team, had amazing individual skills. During warm-ups the fans cheered as their team showed off with trick after trick.

Builder: And the other team?

Director: They went about their pre-game drills methodically. No showing off. No fancy tricks. And it wasn't that they were holding back. They didn't have the tricks.

Builder: What did they have?

Director: Coordinated attack and defense.

Builder: Which the other team lacked.

Director: Yes.

Senator: What happened when they played?

Director: The visiting team crushed the home team. Yes, the latter scored some incredible goals. But they didn't stand a chance.

Builder: So what's your point? If you can't coordinate, you usually lose? And the bad can't coordinate like the good? Then I must be very good indeed!

Senator: How so?

Builder: I personally coordinate my armies of workers. And we always win.

Senator: Yes, but coordination isn't enough.

Builder: Of course it's not enough. But what do you have in mind?

Senator: More than being coordinated, you need to be clear.

Builder: Clear?

Senator: In conscience.

— Conscience

Builder: Leave it to you to bring that up. You'd better explain.

Senator: Do you agree a bad conscience saps your strength?

Builder: I do. And that's good reason to have no conscience at all.

Senator: Yes, yes. But a good conscience gives you strength.

Builder: Does it? I'm sure you think it does. Because, believe it or not, I do think people like you need to feel 'good' about yourselves. And that's what a conscience can do.

Senator: What's wrong with feeling good?

Builder: Oh, it's fine to feel good—so long as you're not blind, which is what too much feeling good can make you.

Director: Can too much feeling bad make you blind, as well?

Builder: Yes.

Director: But just enough feeling bad makes you see?

Builder: That's right.

Director: What can a bad conscience see?

Builder: It can see the good better than a good conscience can see the bad.

Director: How?

Builder: The good aren't a problem for the bad. They're just in the way.

Director: But the bad are a problem for the good?

Builder: They are. The good can't understand why someone would ever be bad.

Director: But the bad know why someone would be good?

Builder: Of course.

Senator: I don't think they understand the good. If they did, they'd be good, too.

Director: Understanding the good is enough to make you good?

Senator: No, being good is the only way to understand the good.

Director: So the good can't understand the bad, and the bad can't understand the good.

Senator: Right. Both are blind here.

Builder: That's why it's best to be neither bad nor good. From that position you can understand both. And this gives you power.

Director: But what kind of conscience do the neither bad nor good have? A neutral conscience?

Builder: There's nothing wrong with that.

Senator: But what does that mean?

Builder: It means you think neither well nor poorly of yourself.

Senator: Do the bad really think poorly of themselves?

Builder: The bad? Yes. But the truly bad? No.

Director: And the truly good?

Builder: No one thinks as poorly of themselves.

Director: Why?

Builder: Because their standards are impossibly high.

Senator: You'd rather they have lower standards?

Builder: And not cripple themselves and those around them? Of course.

Senator: Then what's best? Having no standards at all?

Builder: No, it takes just the right standard to thrive.

Senator: Not too high and not too low?

Builder: Yes.

Director: So what's just right?

Builder: You honestly want to know?

Director: I want to know.

Builder: Just right is doing neither harm nor good.

Senator: What? How can you say just right is doing no good? What's right about that?

Builder: Oh, relax. Tell me. What does it mean to do good?

Senator: To help our fellow women and men.

Builder: Yes, our fellow women and men. And what if they're no good? Do we help them then?

Senator: We help all we can.

Builder: Why?

Senator: Because then they're better off than they were.

Builder: Better off, or better?

Senator: We can say they're better than they were.

Builder: You think by helping you can make someone better? That's arrogant, you know.

Senator: Some people are bad because no one believes in them.

Builder: And that's how you make someone good? By believing in them?

Senator: Do you know of another way?

Builder: There's no making someone bad or good. People are the way they are.

Director: And the sooner we accept that fact, the better?

Builder: Precisely.

Director: You don't believe in second chances?

Builder: A chance for the bad to be good? I'll grant you that if you grant me a chance for the good to be bad.

Director: Can bad or good become neither bad nor good?

Builder: No.

Senator: Why not?

Builder: You have to be born that way.

Senator: And you were born neutral.

Builder: Yes, just as you were born good.

Senator: And Director?

Builder: He's with me.

— The Good

Senator: Are you neutral, Director, as far as good and bad go?

Director: I'm with the good.

Builder: And why is that?

Senator: Why is anyone with the good? They know it's best.

Builder: I think Director sides with the good because he thinks they tend to have more power.

Director: I'd side with them even if they didn't.

Builder: Like under a tyranny?

Director: Tyranny isn't a legitimate form of government.

Builder: What's your point?

Director: Legitimacy is a power. And the good are legitimate.

Senator: He's saying tyranny can't last. The good take back the state.

Builder: It can last longer than you think. Besides, legitimacy alone never won back any state. That takes certain means, which if used, render you less than good.

Director: I don't know about that. But don't you agree that the good, over time, tend to wield more power than the bad, the tyrannical?

Builder: It all depends. But you surprise me. Do you have some sort of political faith in the good?

Director: I can only tell you what I've observed.

Builder: Then you and I aren't looking at the same set of facts.

Senator: The fact in a democracy is that the people are the good.

Builder: You think they're always good?

Senator: We have to keep them good.

Builder: There's your arrogance again. But if we can keep them good, can we make them good when they're not?

Senator: We can create circumstances that foster goodness.

Director: Does that go for other types of rule, other than democracy?

Senator: Can rulers start out bad and then turn good?

Director: Yes. Can they start out in crime? Like treason against the motherland. A revolution, let's say.

Builder: They turn 'good' when they succeed.

Senator: When do they succeed?

Builder: Usually? When the old rulers are rotten to the core.

Director: How does the rot begin?

Builder: There are many ways to rot. But my favorite is in a democracy, when the good start to hate one another.

Senator: Hate rots the soul. And when the soul is rotten it's weak. And then the bad slips in.

Builder: Bad things slip into the soul, or the bad slip into power? With the latter, I think it's less a matter of 'bad' than illegitimate.

Director: Illegitimate concerning the legal, or something more?

Builder: Concerning the legal, yes. But also something more. Tradition, convention.

Senator: Are you saying the new isn't legitimate?

Builder: Not unless newness is the convention, or certain people have an interest in the new.

Senator: You're probably right. But there's more to say about the good hating one another.

Builder: What should we say?

Senator: When they hate they start to call each other bad.

Builder: They certainly do. And then the people divide.

Senator: Divide in a hardened sort of way.

Builder: Yes. Then after a while, to many, all the good seem bad.

Senator: And then the illegitimate might seem alright. But, still, the good must call them bad.

Builder: They do. They call everyone bad who doesn't belong to their clique. But by now people no longer know what to think.

Senator: They're willing to try something new and hope for the best.

Builder: Yes, they blindly put hope in change. They trust the illegitimate. They give them power.

Director: So how can the good turn things around?

Builder: It's very hard. The illegitimate, now somewhat legit, must make a great mistake, or lots and lots of little mistakes. Probably both. And then the good must be ready to act.

— Neutral

Director: Act to take power themselves? Or act on behalf of another?

Senator: Why would they act on behalf of another?

Builder: Because many still think they're bad.

Director: So the question is who, besides the good, wields power best?

Builder: The neutral wield power best.

Senator: Why?

Builder: Because they're free of prejudice.

Senator: No one is free of prejudice. They might insist they're neutral, but they have a certain bias.

Builder: That's why we aim for those who are neutral enough.

Senator: And who would be neutral enough in all this but the young, the untarnished?

Builder: Oh, Senator. The young combine prejudice and passion like no others can. They're hardly neutral.

Senator: So we have to rely on people like you?

Builder: Yes.

Senator: Tell us how you'd get into power.

Builder: Through manipulation, how else?

Director: And, over time, as things settle, you become the new good?

Builder: Of course. The manipulations are hidden away and forgotten. And then, with some time, as you suggest—the neutral are good. That's how things work. That's how they've always worked.

Senator: That's the most cynical thing I've heard you say.

Director: Builder, do the neutral magically become good? Just through the passage of time?

Builder: Don't underestimate the power of the passage of time. But, no. I know what you mean. There's no magic.

Senator: Then what is there?

Builder: You have to allow yourself...

Senator: Allow yourself?

Builder: ...to be manipulated by the good.

Director: That seems to leave a bad taste in your mouth.

Builder: And it does.

Senator: Hold on. You manipulate and then you're manipulated in turn?

Builder: That's the way of the good. Coordination, we might call it. So if you want to blend in....

Senator: But manipulation is manipulation. How can you lead when you're under control?

Builder: You let go of all the less consequential things. This leaves you free for what counts.

Senator: I don't believe it. The good want more than that.

Builder: Oh, you might be surprised. The good will give the neutral more and more power.

Senator: Why would they do that?

Builder: They know the neutral, soon to be good, steer best in dangerous times.

Senator: How do they know that?

Builder: The neutral relish what no one else can stomach.

Senator: Are the others afraid?

Builder: Yes, most of them. But not the fools. They think they know best.

Senator: What do you do with them?

Builder: Give them a taste of power to keep them busy and shuffle them out of the way.

Senator: Cynical, again.

Builder: Then you'll really like this.

Senator: What?

Builder: I lied about becoming good.

Senator: You only seem good.

Builder: Yes, and I let the good think they can manipulate me. Until....

Senator: You have all the power you need.

Builder: Right.

Senator: But why would you do all this?

Builder: Why? Because I have a tyrannical soul.

— Tyranny

Director: What is tyranny?

Builder: Oh, you know what it is.

Director: Strong man rule?

Builder: Don't count out the women.

Director: Can we settle on this? Rule by one who has absolute power without legal right.

Senator: No. There can be more than one tyrant in a land. Don't you agree?

Builder: They'll all compete until there's only one.

Director: Is that oneness, that complete concentration of power, in the nature of tyranny?

Builder: Of course.

Senator: But haven't you ever heard of petty tyrants?

Builder: Yes, but they always take as much power as they can get. It's just, for whatever reason, they can only take so much.

Senator: Take as in appropriate, or take as in bear?

Builder: A good question.

Director: Why do you think tyrants love to take?

Senator: They never really learned to share.

Builder: You really think it's that simple?

Senator: Yes, I do. Or if they share, it's with an ulterior motive.

Builder: That's true. But I'm wondering about something in Director's definition. Absolute power, without legal right.

Director: What's to wonder?

Builder: It suggests there can be absolute power, with legal right.

Senator: We usually think of that as an absolute monarchy.

Builder: Yes, and if a tyrant comes to power without legal right, but then manages to acquire it....

Senator: What are you suggesting? That a vote of the people can make a tyranny a monarchy?

Builder: In the fading echoes of a democracy? Why not?

Director: Can this happen under other forms of government?

Builder: Can tyrants rise to power and then become legitimate there? Sure.

Director: How?

Builder: Let's hear what Senator has to say.

Senator: Well, the tyrant would have to persuade –

Builder: Ha, ha. Persuade.

Senator:—persuade those who can confer legitimacy, to grant it to her or him.

Director: Can you imagine anyone but the people holding that power?

Senator: We just have to look through history.

Builder: Yes, and when we do, we'll see that the concept of 'the people' changes with time.

Director: Are you saying the people have always been the source of legitimacy?

Builder: No, of course not. But they are today. And there are two factors in play.

Director: What two?

Builder: There's the power of the people, and then there's their size.

Senator: Size as in who makes up the people?

Builder: Yes.

Director: Can you give us an example of a change in size?

Builder: Slaves. They weren't part of the people. When they were freed the people grew.

Director: And what about the people's power?

Builder: It's harder to give an example here. Suffice it to say, the people's power is often nominal at best, with the real power elsewhere.

Senator: But sometimes the people have real power.

Builder: Yes, but usually not for long.

Director: So what are you saying, Builder? Power and size can shrink and grow?

Builder: That's right.

Director: Then we have to be careful when we look to history.

Senator: What do you mean?

Director: Well, for instance, we might find a people who hold power. But neither this people nor its power are as we understand them today.

Builder: A very good point.

Senator: But size is power today.

Builder: That's open to some debate.

Senator: Regardless, the point is that the good might split on this. Some want the people to shrink, some want the people to grow.

Director: Who wants the people to grow?

Senator: Those who believe democracy is good.

Builder: And who wants the people to shrink?

Senator: Those who believe in aristocracy.

Builder: Oh, you're aiming too high. Who wants the people to grow? Those who benefit from this. Who wants them to shrink? The same.

Director: What kind of benefits do you have in mind?

Builder: It could be anything, however petty you might imagine. Who can say?

Director: How about an example?

Builder: A young man dreams of holding office one day. He believes only the few will recognize his noble worth. And so he wants to shrink the people.

Director: You call that petty? Can you give us an example of something petty, Senator?

Senator: Someone sells goods to someone who wants to shrink the people. So our seller decides it's good to shrink the people, too—good for business, that is.

Director: How about on the other side?

Senator: Growing the people? A young man falls in love with a young woman who believes in expansion. He comes to believe in expansion, too.

Director: And a less noble motivation?

Senator: I'm having a hard time thinking of one.

Builder: That's because of your politics. Here's an example. A senator knows that if the base grows he or she will get more votes—because he or she is on the right side of the issue.

Director: Is that the only petty interest someone could have in expansion?

Builder: Of course not.

Senator: Name another.

Builder: Well....

Senator: Ha! You can't!

Builder: My mind isn't used to dwelling on the petty.

Senator: Nor is it used to dwelling on the noble.

Director: However that may be, let's get back to tyranny. Can we agree there are at least three sorts? Tyranny of the many, tyranny of the few, and tyranny of the one.

Builder: Yes, and they all tend toward tyranny of the one.

Senator: So if forced to choose, which would be least bad?

Builder: The best of bad? That's the many.

— The Many

Director: Why are the many least bad?

Builder: Because they tend to undermine themselves.

Senator: What do you mean?

Builder: They never fully concentrate or coordinate their power. There are too many currents, or factions.

Director: And if they coordinate and concentrate?

Builder: They become worse.

Senator: Why?

Builder: They get used to getting their way.

Senator: But isn't that good?

Builder: Your question shows your ignorance. What happens when we're used to getting anything we want, good or bad?

Senator: I don't know. What?

Builder: We grow corrupt. And once corrupt, we stay corrupt. Take it from me.

Director: So what can we do?

Builder: Divide the many and stand them as long as we can, then replace them with the few.

Senator: The few remaining good?

Builder: Yes, whatever you take 'good' to mean.

Director: How long can these good hold out?

Builder: It all depends.

Director: On what?

Builder: How much force they command.

Senator: But using force against the many makes the few tyrannical themselves. Doesn't it?

Builder: Glad to see you're catching on.

Director: What happens then?

Builder: When they're corrupt, which is to say tyrannical? It's time for the tyranny of one.

Senator: Builder's cue to step on stage.

Director: When the tyrant steps in, is it usually from within the few?

Builder: No, it's almost always from without.

Senator: Why?

Builder: Because he or she makes an appeal to the many.

Senator: The corrupted many, the many the few hold down.

Builder: Yes.

Director: To what in the many does the tyrant appeal?

Builder: Their hatred of the few.

Director: And to put these few down, the tyrant organizes the people's force?

Builder: To good effect.

Director: Yes, but how?

Builder: It's simple. He or she gets rid of the weaker factions and combines the strong.

Senator: But what do the people hope to get, aside from deposing the few?

Builder: What do you want me to say? They want their goodness again?

Senator: Just tell us what they want.

Builder: Reward.

— Punish, Reward

Director: What kind of reward?

Builder: Money is the greatest. Positions and titles are next. And I'm sure you can imagine many lesser things, too.

Director: Like reserved parking spots at the office?

Builder: Ha, ha. Yes.

Director: You have the kind of power it takes for these things.

Builder: I do.

Director: Is that your only power? To reward?

Builder: No, it's in my power to punish, as well.

Director: So you might take away money, take away positions and titles, take away parking spots.

Builder: If it comes to that, I usually just take away the person's job.

Director: Why?

Builder: Don't you know the old saying? If you harm someone, kill them, too.

Director: Because they might find a way to take revenge?

Builder: Yes. Or, in my case, they might spread malcontent.

Director: And firing serves to spread some fear.

Builder: Yes, and it's healthy.

Senator: Why is fear healthy?

Builder: It keeps people honest.

Senator: They're only honest because they're afraid?

Builder: For many? That's right.

Director: But what about those who don't need fear to be honest?

Builder: They have nothing to fear from me. Well, mostly nothing.

Director: Their virtue protects them from harm?

Builder: Virtue. Sure.

Senator: And what virtue protects you from harm?

Builder: My wise use of power.

Director: Knowing when to punish and when to reward.

Builder: Exactly.

Director: But how hard is it to know that? You punish when someone doesn't do well. You reward when someone does.

Builder: Yes, but you need to know when to hold back.

Director: Hold back in punishment?

Builder: Or in reward.

Director: Tell us when you hold back with each.

Builder: With punishment? Say someone makes an honest mistake. You should forgive them that. They still might be a good employee.

Director: But?

Builder: But if they err out of laziness you need to strike some fear into them.

Director: Fear counters laziness nicely.

Builder: Yes. And if they don't respond well to the fear, you get rid of them.

Director: Okay. And what about holding back in reward?

Builder: Reward doesn't mean anything if you give it out too freely. So only exceptional virtue should find its reward.

Senator: And this is your management philosophy.

Builder: It's the only true philosophy there's ever been. Even parents use it on kids. Good parents, at any rate. You should use it on your staff.

Senator: And while I'm at it, why not on the electorate?

Builder: Ha, ha. Because they should use it on you.

— Courage and Hate

Director: Why are we calling this method a philosophy?

Builder: Because that's what it is.

Director: Is it? It seems more like an attempt at wisdom, to me.

Builder: Oh, fine. We'll be particular, philosopher. But why an attempt? What other wisdom is there when it comes to these things? I'm expressing the basics—love of reward and fear of punishment.

Director: And what of their opposites?

Builder: What of them?

Director: What's the opposite of love?

Builder: Hate.

Director: And what's the opposite of fear?

Builder: Courage.

Director: Do you want your employees to have courage and hate?

Builder: It depends.

Director: On what?

Builder: Courage is good, within the limits of sense.

Director: And hate?

Builder: Hate for the competition is good.

Director: So a wise employer promotes both courage, within sense, and hate.

Senator: You can't be serious.

Builder: Why not? What's wrong with courage and hate?

Senator: What's wrong with hate? Are you really asking? Well, knowing you, I think you are!

Builder: Oh, forget about hate. What about courage? Don't you have to be brave enough to do a good job?

Senator: Why do you have to be brave for that?

Builder: Good jobs are often punished. Not by me. But they are.

Senator: Why?

Builder: Who can say? Managers feel threatened by the good work of their subordinates. Can't you imagine things like this? Oh, I'm sorry. You probably can't.

Senator: Why do you say that?

Builder: Your subordinates are too far away from your majestic rank for you to feel any pressure from them.

Senator: And you feel threatened by yours?

Builder: By those closest to me? Only if they receive offers to go off and run other firms. Then they become competition. Competition is always a threat.

Senator: A threat you and your employees love to hate. But tell us. If you don't punish good jobs, why do your employees need courage?

Builder: Because they can't know I won't punish them until after they do the job.

Senator: Well, that makes sense. You create a culture of fear, after all.

Builder: And you know the problem with this, of course.

Senator: There are many problems. What problem do you have in mind?

Builder: People might be afraid to tell me the truth.

Senator: They need courage to speak truth to the boss.

Builder: Right. So I find ways to reward their courage. But I'll tell you something else.

Senator: What, Builder?

Builder: I want employees to direct their hate at me—as well as the competition, of course.

Director: Why hate toward you?

Builder: If they hate me they'll try to show me up by doing excellent work.

Senator: I'm not so sure about that psychology.

Builder: That's why you're not me.

Director: So how does it work?

Builder: Hate spurs them on to prove me wrong about them.

Senator: You think little of them by default?

Builder: Yes, of course.

Senator: And you reward them when they prove you wrong.

Builder: To good effect.

Senator: What good effect? Do they love you then?

Builder: Some do. But I prefer their continued hate.

Senator: Why in the world do you prefer that?

Builder: Their hate keeps me honest, keeps me on my toes.

Senator: You need hate for that? That's what love does for me.

Builder: You overrate love. After all, love is blind. Ha, ha. But hate? That's a clear-eyed reliable thing.

— Vision

Senator: Well, I have to say. I've never heard of an employer who actively wants to be hated.

Director: And yet countless employers act as if that's exactly what they want.

Senator: True enough. Builder, why do you think they act that way?

Builder: Many of them? They're on the defensive.

Senator: And we hate those who defend themselves?

Builder: When the defense is at our expense? Yes, of course. What they need to do is attack.

Senator: And then they won't be hated?

Builder: Of course not. But then the hate will be put to better use. It sharpens the attack.

Senator: But why attack?

Builder: Because it's better to attack than defend.

Senator: Why?

Builder: If you don't know, I can't say.

Director: Builder, does it take more to attack than defend?

Builder: Of course it does. It takes more vision.

Senator: Vision? How so?

Builder: When you attack, you have to see all the various possibilities and choose your opportunity well. When you defend, there's usually not much choice. So what does this say about you?

Senator: What do you mean?

Builder: Do you have the vision it takes to attack your enemies?

Senator: What enemies?

Builder: My point exactly.

Director: Senator, don't you have enemies in the senate?

Senator: It doesn't work like that.

Director: How does it work?

Senator: The senate is a collegial body. We work together, despite our differences.

Builder: When's the last time that worked out?

Senator: We can't get anything done without working together.

Builder: Like I said. When's the last time that worked out? But what about my money?

Senator: What about it?

Builder: When I give money to your party, I want to see you attack the other side.

Senator: Those kinds of attack don't take much vision. In fact, nearly all types of attack take very little vision.

Director: What does take vision?

Senator: Knowing how things can and should be.

Builder: But what if you have two visions on this? One for the voters to see, and one you keep to yourself.

Senator: I know people who see that way. It's all an act until they're behind closed doors. And even then....

Director: You can't trust them?

Senator: Of course you can't.

Builder: But the voters, they can trust you.

Senator: I have one vision for all to see.

Director: Do any of your colleagues share this vision?

Senator: A few of them do, on certain points.

Director: And the rest?

Senator: They largely disagree.

Builder: So what can you do? Don't you need their support to get anything done?

Senator: I do. But, Builder, you know politics is compromise. What can I say?

Builder: You don't have to compromise—if you're a tyrant.

Director: Is that the best part of tyranny? But tell us this. If the people hate compromise, hate it with a passion, do they long for a tyrant to step in and set things straight?

Builder: They might not know that's what they long for, but they long for it nonetheless.

Senator: But is the tyrant's vision true?

Builder: What does that mean? Forget about true. The vision is one.

Director: Really? Tyrants are consistent?

Builder: They try to keep things very simple. And when you do that you often seem consistent. But their true consistency is that they only look out for themselves.

Director: So they can be inconsistent in all things, but so long as they look out for themselves...

Builder: ...they're consistent. Yes. And that's the vision they keep to themselves. Others can sense this consistency, this inner power—and it attracts.

Senator: Sure, it attracts a certain kind of crowd.

Director: Do you think it's bad for this crowd to come together?

Senator: In support of a tyrant? There's nothing worse.

— Tyranny 2

Director: Not even the tyrant her- or himself?

Senator: They're equally bad. The supporters are the tyrant's extended will.

Director: And the tyrant has a consistent will.

Senator: Yes, the tyrant is a slave to power. It's all about that, whatever the cost—including inconsistencies that others must swallow.

Director: Would you say a tyrant is consistently inconsistent to others?

Senator: Yes.

Director: Then tell us this. Is power always at a cost to others?

Senator: My power never is.

Builder: That's because you have so little.

Senator: And what about your power?

Builder: I'm closer to a tyrant than you think.

Senator: Don't presume what I think.

Builder: Oh, Senator, then let me tell you how close I am. Just look how I live. I'm rich far beyond my juvenile dreams. I command armies of workers in many lands. The skies are filled with monuments to me. I sway legislation and answer to no one but myself.

Director: You sound better off than any tyrant that ever was.

Builder: It's true.

Senator: Then what's the difference between tyrants of old and you?

Builder: They didn't have people like you to support them.

Senator: What do you mean?

Builder: I don't want to rule in a general sense. I rule myself and my affairs. As for the rest? Honestly? I couldn't care less.

Senator: You leave the care to me. But I can pass laws to regulate you.

Builder: You and your closest senator friends? I'll just give more to them and we'll see what we see.

Director: And you'll be consistent in this.

Builder: Of course I will. Like I said, it's all about me and my affairs. I'll promote myself and them however I see fit. Oh, and Senator—I obey the laws. That's how the tyrants of old and I differ, you see.

Senator: That's because the laws are in your favor.

Builder: And whose fault is that?

— Law

Director: What does it mean to believe in the rule of law?

Senator: You believe that law should reign supreme. And that everyone should be subject.

Director: What does that mean for those who make the law?

Senator: They have a very serious responsibility.

Director: And for those who execute the law?

Senator: The same.

Director: And for those who interpret the law?

Senator: It's just like it is for the others.

Director: Is law opposed to tyranny?

Senator: Of course it is.

Director: Then tell me. How do all these serious minded people let tyrants like Builder slip through?

Senator: We don't like to interfere with private enterprise.

Director: So if Builder wants to strike fear into the hearts of his employees, he can.

Senator: Unless he goes too far? Yes.

Director: And there's nothing you can do to stop him?

Senator: Like I said, we don't like to interfere.

Director: Why?

Senator: Because of the risk.

Director: What risk?

Builder: I'll tell you what risk. If the government is everywhere, and one day it turns tyrannical, there's no safe retreat.

Director: What would cause the government to turn tyrannical?

Builder: What causes anyone to turn tyrannical? They have tyrannical tendencies, Director. We all do. All we need is a chance.

Senator: Not all of us do. I don't have a tyrannical bone in my body.

Builder: Maybe you're the exception that proves the rule.

Director: But don't tyrants compete and serve as a check on one another?

Builder: Say more.

Director: Would a tyrant in government tolerate a tyrant in business?

Builder: Not if they could help it.

Director: Putting the business tyrant down would enhance the government tyrant's authority?

Builder: Yes.

Director: And authority is something tyrants want?

Builder: Certainly.

Director: So if a business tyrant could put a government tyrant down, they would?

Builder: I've done that. And it's a benefit to all.

Director: Did it enhanced your power?

Builder: It did.

Senator: But if you do things like this, who checks you?

Builder: I check me.

Senator: The law will check you, if I have any say.

Builder: And I will check the law. But there's no 'if' that I have say.

— Checks

Senator: I know how you check the law. You pay my party to loosen its restrictions.

Builder: I pay the other party, too, if that's any consolation.

Director: Senator, do you compete with Builder?

Senator: I have no desire to be a tyrant.

Builder: You don't have to be. The laws you pass can play the tyrant well enough.

Senator: Laws can be tyrants? Ha, ha.

Builder: Of course they can! Where do you think frustrated legislative tyrants impose their will? On the law!

Senator: Sometimes they pass laws they don't like.

Director: Why do they pass them?

Senator: The people's will for them is strong.

Builder: Then the people are tyrants imposing their will on the law.

Senator: Give us an example of a tyrannical law.

Builder: Confiscatory taxes on businesses and the rich.

Senator: Well....

Builder: You can't deny it! What do you think, Director?

Director: I think there can be other tyrannical laws, laws that don't have to do with money.

Senator: Name such a law.

Director: A law that prevents people from being what they are.

Builder: You see? Tyranny!

Senator: So if a law prevents a natural born killer from killing, it's tyrannical?

Builder: Oh, he doesn't mean that. He means something like this. At heart I'm a powerful man. If the laws get in the way of my being what I am, they're tyrannical. Right?

Senator: Very funny.

Builder: What are you, Director, that the laws might suppress?

Director: I'm a philosopher. And the laws might silence me.

Senator: Why would they silence you?

Director: Because they don't like the questions I raise.

Senator: Questions about the laws? But then you're a good check on them.

Builder: And the laws want to be a good check on him!

Director: Yes, but I'm no expert in the law.

Builder: What are you an expert in?

Director: Questions. Questions about all sorts of things—even power, too.

Senator: And these questions don't have to do with law?

Director: Why, no. Many of them have to do with law. But, as I've said, I'm not an expert here.

Builder: Oh, don't be falsely modest. I know what you think you are.

Director: Tell me what I think I am.

Builder: You think you're inspiration—for givers of law.

— Inspiration

Director: What does it mean to inspire?

Builder: To give them ideas.

Director: Oh, I think they have plenty of ideas on their own.

Builder: Yes, but good ideas?

Director: What good ideas could I give?

Builder: Ideas for non-tyrannical laws. Or you could do one better. Come help me get rid of tyrannical laws.

Senator: How is he supposed to do that?

Builder: He can get you and your friends to lower my taxes. I'd even give money to the cause!

Senator: Director, how would you define tyranny in law?

Director: In a very broad sense? How's this? It's force without persuasion.

Builder: What kind of definition is that? We don't persuade thieves, for instance, to go to jail. We force them. Does that make us tyrants? No.

Director: Then what is tyranny in law?

Builder: It's cruelty. That's the only thing that matters.

Senator: So a cruel law is a tyrannical law.

Builder: Yes.

Director: What inspires someone to be cruel?

Builder: Oh, who can say? Ambition? Impatience? Pain? Revenge? Justice, even? But I don't know that 'inspires' is the right word.

Director: What is the right word?

Builder: These things can drive, drive a person to be cruel.

— The Tyrant in Me

Director: How do you know this, Builder?

Builder: At times I'm in touch with the tyrant in me.

Senator: At times?

Builder: No one can be wholly tyrannical, cruel all the time.

Director: Why not?

Builder: Because you need allies, supporters.

Director: But people can ally and support out of fear, no?

Builder: Well, that's true. And what's more reliable than fear?

Senator: Fear is the drive of those you rule.

Builder: But it can paralyze, too. But I'll tell you something. I don't inspire fear in my equals.

Senator: Tyrants have equals?

Builder: They'd like to, at least.

Director: You'd really like to have equals?

Builder: I really would.

Director: Then I don't see how you can be a tyrant. Tyrants isolate themselves. There can only be one. Didn't you know?

Builder: I don't know that they isolate themselves. I think circumstances conspire to isolate them.

Director: And they would get out, lose their tyrannical drive, if only they could?

Builder: But they can't. And that's the tragedy of tyranny.

Senator: Oh, stop feeling sorry for yourself. You need friends. And good friends are hard to find—for everyone. Tyrants aren't unique in this.

Builder: But let me tell you the truth. The longing that would-be tyrants have for friends, it evolves into tyranny.

Senator: That's nonsense, and you know it.

Director: Why would it evolve that way?

Builder: Because when you have no friends, it drives you to be cruel.

Director: And you're not talking about any old friend. You're talking about something special?

Builder: A true friend, Director. That's what a tyrant needs.

Director: So why not give up tyranny and spend your time looking for friends?

Builder: Tyranny, once taken up, is very hard, if not impossible, to put down.

Director: Why?

Builder: Because once people stop fearing you, they come to hate.

Senator: I thought hate was reliable, something you want.

Director: Yes, but now he's speaking of something more.

Builder: I am. Total hate. Hate you can't rein in.

Senator: And when you achieve this hate?

Builder: You might as well be dead.

— Death

Director: Do tyrants fear death?

Builder: Yes and no.

Director: Why yes?

Builder: Everyone fears death to some degree.

Director: And tyrants fear plots against their life?

Builder: Of course.

Director: Even tyrants like you?

Builder: I've made enemies in my time.

Director: Enemies enough to kill?

Builder: I don't know. I think there's a chance.

Director: Hmm. But you also said tyrants don't fear death.

Builder: Death is the tyrant's only release.

Senator: That sounds awful.

Builder: It is what it is.

Senator: Then why would anyone want to be a tyrant?

Builder: Honestly? You get into it before you know any better.

Director: If potential tyrants knew what tyranny is, they wouldn't become tyrants?

Builder: Yes, but let's be blunt. If everyone knew what life is, they wouldn't bother to live.

Senator: That's not true.

Builder: That's because you never lost your illusions.

Director: Loss of illusions makes us want to die?

Builder: Or live the only possible honest way.

Director: The way of the tyrant.

Builder: Yes.

Senator: This is nonsense.

Builder: Why? Life is all about power, power relations, to put it in so many words. So the only honest pursuit is to gain more power. That's what a tyrant does. Anything else is a lie.

Senator: Then I'd be happy to live my lies.

Builder: That's the only possible honest retort. And you, Director, do you seek more power or do you lie to yourself?

Director: Neither. I found another way.

Senator: What way?

Director: Philosophy.

Builder: So tell us about philosophy.

Director: Haven't you heard philosophy is learning to die?

Senator: I've heard that. Is it true?

Director: As true as anything we're saying here today.

Builder: How does asking questions teach you to die?

Director: I don't have a good answer for that.

Builder: Then give us a bad one.

Director: I wish I could.

Builder: So you'll just make a statement you can't back up?

Director: Oh, I can back it up. Just not in so many words.

— Words

Builder: I like that, you know. Not relying on words.

Director: But I do rely on words. Just not so many.

Senator: You prove your point over time.

Director: Yes.

Builder: But I know you. You prove through deeds, as well.

Director: Of course I do.

Senator: Words without deeds mean nothing.

Director: Yes, Senator. But we should note that words can be deeds.

Builder: How?

Director: When they're spoken to just the right person at just the right time.

Senator: You have a point. When I say just the right things at just the right time to the people, there's a powerful effect.

Director: Builder, you like effects. And yet you never make public speeches.

Builder: What would be the point? I talk one-on-one to those I need.

Senator: So do I. But I also speak to the public at large.

Builder: You speak to the public because you're beholden to them.

Senator: Or maybe it's because I have more power with them than you do.

Builder: 'With' them? Not 'over' them?

Senator: With them. Together we have power. And so you can see, I'm no tyrant.

Director: And your words reflect this truth.

Senator: Of course they do. My language includes, includes the people.

Director: And Builder's words exclude?

Senator: Except when they're spinning a web of fear.

Builder: Oh, you make me sound so bad. But you too use fear, good Senator.

Senator: How?

Builder: You fear the opposing party. And you teach your people this fear. In fact, that's been a major force in all your campaigns. I've seen it with my own eyes.

Senator: I teach more hope than fear.

Builder: And there's some power in hopeful words. But there's nothing quite like fear.

— Hope

Director: What is it about fear?

Builder: Hope can leave you in an instant. That's not generally so with fear. Fear tends to linger.

Senator: But hope can drive away fear.

Builder: Sure. But if you lose your hope, you're left with the fear.

Director: What can make hope last as long as fear?

Senator: I'll tell you. Hope gains in power as we grow in faith.

Director: Strong faith drives away fear?

Senator: Of course it does.

Director: Builder, do you hire those with strong faith?

Builder: You're wondering because they might be immune to my tyranny? Sure, I hire those with faith.

Senator: But how do you control them?

Builder: Just because you're not afraid doesn't mean you won't obey.

Director: Can you say more?

Builder: Too much faith makes you complacent where you are. You don't take action. You just believe.

Senator: You mean, faith makes people sheep.

Builder: Yes, and I'm their shepherd. Ha, ha.

Director: But faith has launched many a bold attack.

Builder: I should have been clear. There are two sorts of faith—bold and meek.

Senator: And you only hire the meek?

Builder: Generally, but not as a rule. I hire the bold that I can direct toward my enemies.

Senator: What makes them want to attack?

Builder: They're hopeful they'll win—and that I'm good for their reward.

Director: Do you ever inspire hope with the meek?

Builder: Why would I do that?

Director: You win their best efforts that way.

Builder: Yes, yes. But their best efforts usually aren't that great. It's hardly worth the trouble.

Senator: I don't believe it.

Builder: Look, do you want to know the real problem? Their hope limits my options. Their fear gives me scope.

Senator: You're not afraid of talking like this?

Builder: What's to fear? You'll tell the people who fear me that I seek to cause fear? That's a good one, Senator. But I can see why you're concerned.

Senator: Oh? Why is that?

Builder: Because hope is your only choice.

Senator: That's not true.

Builder: What are you going to do? Make your electors afraid of you?

Senator: I can make others afraid.

Builder: Who, other senators?

Senator: No, people like you.

Builder: Hope to the people and fear to the tyrants?

Senator: Don't you think that's what the people want?

Builder: Sure, that's what they want. Maybe you're not as helpless as I thought. But, in the end, you have to do what they want. I, I do what I like—unless you can stop me. But remember, I can give lots of money to your peers.

Senator: Director, how is it with you?

Director: With me? What fear do I inspire?

Senator: What hope do you inspire?

Builder: He's not in that business. So ask him this. What is it you inspire, Director?

Director: I like to inspire thought.

— Thought

Builder: Why inspire that?

Director: Because thought can make the world a better place.

Builder: Oh no! Can it be? You're just another idealist!

Director: I'm realistic about how many will actually think.

Builder: One in ten?

Director: Fewer.

Senator: One in a hundred?

Director: Fewer.

Builder: One in a thousand.

Director: Close. One in ten thousand.

Builder: Ha, ha. I'm glad you're joking with me. So tell me. How many will actually think things through?

Director: Think things through all the way? One in a billion.

Builder: So, what, seven or ten people in the world today have thought things all the way through? Well, if I'm one, and you're two, where are the others?

Director: Oh, I'm not saying I'm one.

Builder: But you think I am?

Director: No, I don't. Sorry.

Builder: How do you know I haven't thought it all through?

Director: Because you're still thinking.

Builder: True. I think. And so do you. But why only seven or ten in the whole world?

Director: This is what I've learned from study of the past.

Senator: History really says the world has only known ten or so at a time who've thought it all through?

Director: Well, maybe it's more like thirty.

Builder: Thirty? Why not a hundred?

Director: Sure, we can say a hundred. It doesn't much change the odds.

Builder: No, it doesn't. But this joke of yours is wearing thin. What does it mean to think things all the way through?

Director: To run out of things to think.

Builder: No, that never happens.

Director: But I think it does, for some.

Builder: How can you be sure?

Director: They write books, give lectures, have a teaching.

Senator: You can't have a teaching unless you think things all the way through?

Director: Not a final teaching.

Builder: A final teaching? That's a laugh.

Director: You don't think there are those who've taught these things?

Builder: No, I suppose you have a point. But we should be opposed to these final teachers.

Senator: Why?

Builder: Because anything that puts an end to thought is false.

Senator: Even if the teaching is true?

Builder: You can teach the truth about apples. But if you ignore the other fruits, your teaching is incomplete.

Senator: Not if all you care about is apples.

Builder: All I can say is then you miss out. Don't you agree, Director?

Director: I love apples. But I like a good mango now and then, too.

Builder: And that's the point.

Senator: But what if someone teaches the truth about all fruit?

Builder: There are a lot of fruits in the world—to say nothing of all the vegetables. You need to teach the truth about them, as well, you know.

Senator: So what are you saying? You need to know all things? That's impossible.

Director: And yet there are those who teach the total, final truth.

Senator: Even though they haven't thought all things through.

Director: Even though.

Senator: They just think they have.

Director: Yes.

Senator: What does their teaching accomplish?

Director: It seeks to snuff out thought. And often does.

Senator: But if you think you've thought it all through, why not encourage others to do the same?

Director: Because what you found with your thought seemed bleak.

— Color

Builder: I know what they find.

Senator: What?

Builder: That all things come into being then die. A mountain rises, exists for a while, then dies—exists no more. The sun exists but one day burns itself out. It dies. Nothing excepted.

Director: And so anything goes.

Builder: You've seen what I see.

Senator: But that's not what Director thinks.

Director: What do I think?

Senator: You believe in the great cycle of being.

Builder: Oh, that's not what he believes.

Senator: Then what does he believe?

Builder: As he said—that anything goes.

Director: I don't believe that.

Senator: So what do you believe?

Director: That we should add color to life.

Builder: How is that any different than believing anything goes?

Director: Not everything brings color.

Senator: He's got you there.

Builder: So what brings color?

Director: For one? Mirth.

Senator: Oh, he's really got you there!

Builder: Bah. I don't believe in mirth. Those who believe in mirth are fools.

Director: Yes, but I don't believe in mirth. I know, know mirth adds color, adds life.

Senator: Color is life?

Director: Color is life.

Builder: What rot are you talking? You'd better find something other than mirth.

Director: I have. Love.

Senator: Ah! He's absolutely right! Love no doubt adds color.

Builder: Mirth, love—what else?

Director: That's not enough for now?

Builder: Talk of mirth brings tragedy to mind.

Senator: Knowing you? Of course it does.

Builder: How can we speak of the comic without speaking of the tragic?

Director: Tragedy adds darker colors to life.

Senator: And the darker colors aren't good.

Builder: I thought all color was good.

Senator: Color is color. But the lighter colors are good. The darker colors are bad.

Builder: For me, the darker colors are good.

Senator: You like tragedy in your life?

Builder: I like a good dark red from time to time.

Senator: We're not talking about your taste in wine.

Builder: No, but I really do. Tragedy. There's beauty in it, you know.

Senator: When it's in your own life, or in the lives of others?

Builder: Wouldn't I be a hypocrite to like it in others' lives but not my own?

Senator: No one likes tragedy in their own life. I don't believe you.

Builder: You haven't dived as deep into life as I have, my friend. But ask Director, if you doubt me.

Director: Builder, I'm not sure what you mean by tragedy.

Builder: Great loss.

Director: Who likes great loss?

Senator: Exactly. I think Builder has nothing to lose. So he really can't imagine loss. Or, in a crazy way, he thinks the possibility of tragedy means he might have something to lose. And he likes that idea, having something to lose.

Builder: Thanks for the psychological evaluation. Remind me to give less to your party next year. But tell us about the brighter colors.

Senator: I can sum them up in a word. Happiness.

— Happiness 2

Builder: So is happiness light pink or sky blue?

Senator: Laugh all you want. But you haven't dived as deep into happiness as I have.

Builder: And when you dove, what did you see?

Senator: I saw what the greatest power on Earth longs to see.

Builder: Which is?

Senator: Power made free.

Builder: Happiness makes power free? But when is power ever a slave?

Senator: When it only believes in itself.

Builder: It should believe in cheery springtime pastels?

Senator: Director, can you help me here?

Director: I can try. No, it shouldn't believe in cheery pastels. But you have power, Builder. What do you believe in?

Builder: I don't believe in any color, if that's what you mean.

Director: Then what?

Builder: I believe in myself. And despite what Senator might think, I'm no slave.

Director: How can you be sure?

Builder: How does a slave know they're a slave?

Senator: They can't do what they like. And you can't do what you like.

Builder: Why not?

Senator: Because you have no choice but to cause fear.

Builder: But how do you know that's not what I like?

Senator: That can't be all you like. Don't you like to be loved?

Builder: I prefer fear.

Senator: Why?

Builder: It gets me what I want.

Senator: I find that hard to believe.

Builder: Believe it or not, it's true.

Senator: Have you ever known happiness?

Builder: Not your kind of happiness, no.

Director: What's your experience of happiness, Senator?

Senator: It sounds so simple to say, but it means the world. Happiness lifts my spirits.

Director: Are high spirits and happiness one and the same?

Senator: Why wouldn't they be?

Builder: Well, I have high spirits when I tyrannize over others. Am I happy then?

Senator: Of course not.

Director: So high spirits and happiness differ?

Senator: Apparently so.

Builder: I think the happy don't have high spirits.

Senator: What do they have?

Builder: An even bearing that makes them feel glad.

Senator: The bearing comes before the feeling?

Builder: Of course it does.

Senator: I don't know about that. I think the feeling creates the bearing. I can carry myself however I will, but that can't make me happy.

Builder: That's because you're weak.

Director: Builder, tell us how carrying yourself a particular way can make you happy if you're strong.

Builder: And give away my secret? Never.

Senator: But you're not happy.

Builder: Happier than you. My power is backed by strength.

Senator: And mine isn't?

Builder: Of course not.

Senator: But if I don't have strength, how do I have power?

Builder: The little power you have you got by making others believe in you.

Senator: Oh, you're impossible. But I'll tell you this. Strength can be nothing but brute force. Power is something more.

Director: Power is a state of mind.

Builder: Yes, exactly so. And without that state of mind, you can be strong like an ox—but have no power at all.

— States of Mind

Senator: Then what's the state of mind that makes the difference here?

Builder: It's a willingness to manipulate others.

Senator: Of course that's what you think. Why do you want to be a puppeteer?

Builder: Because I don't want any strings attached to me. And I like to pull them on others.

Senator: I've seen enough power to know. There are strings attached to all the puppeteers, no matter how clever they think they are.

Builder: And you've pulled no strings in your political life?

Senator: I've pulled enough to want to pull no more.

Builder: Then how do you survive? And note. I give money to your party but not to you.

Senator: Yes, I've noticed. And I understand why. How do I survive? I'm loved by my people and peers.

Builder: And that's better than pulling strings?

Senator: It's more honest.

Builder: I'll tell you what's more honest than that. Fear.

Director: So when we pull strings, we can bring out what we want?

Builder: What do you mean?

Director: Fear, love, hate.

Builder: Yes, depending on your skill.

Senator: Which would you bring out, if you could?

Builder: If I could? Ha, ha. Why don't you guess?

Senator: Fear, with hate a close second.

Builder: And why do you think that is?

Senator: Because you think fear is honest?

Builder: No, it's because fear gets you more for the effort you put in.

Director: What takes the greatest effort, Builder?

Builder: Now it's your turn to guess.

Director: Alright, I'll guess this. Doing all you can to hide that you're the puppeteer.

Builder: Ha! Just so. And do you know why?

Director: It's your turn to explain.

Builder: It's because you don't want to ruin the beautiful effect.

Director: Because puppetry is an art?

Builder: Of course it is!

Director: Hmm.

Builder: What is it?

Director: I'm trying to understand.

Builder: What's to understand?

Director: Is it good to manipulate others?

Builder: But that's the thing! It's not good—it's bad, very bad. Ha, ha. But it feels so good. You know what I mean.

Director: I'm not so sure I do.

Builder: You hide the fact that you manipulate others.

Senator: How does he manipulate others?

Builder: Through words. Shall I tell you how it's done?

Senator: Yes.

Builder: Director makes people question their words. And while they're busy with that, he suggests words of his own.

Senator: To what end?

Builder: To get them to do what he wants. That's how he helped me on that project of mine. He confused people, then suggested what they should do.

Senator: And they were happy to oblige, in order to get out of their difficulty?

Builder: You understand well.

Director: But, Builder, they were confused before I met them.

Builder: Yes, but you brought their confusion to the fore. And then you helped them see their way clear.

Senator: By prompting them to do your bidding?

Builder: Yes, of course.

Senator: And Director was doing your bidding, too?

Builder: No doubt.

Senator: I don't know. I doubt Director does anyone's bidding. He has reasons of his own.

Builder: And yet the work got done. And I intend to hire him for greater things. Wouldn't you like that, Director?

Director: It depends on the job.

Senator: Not used to an answer like that, are you, Builder?

Builder: Who takes an unknown job dealing with greater things? I'll tell you who. Everyone I deal with. But Director likes to feel he's independent.

Senator: He seems independent to me.

Builder: Yes, sure. But have a look at him when the money runs out. His state of mind will differ then.

— Independence

Senator: I think independence, when times are tough, is the greatest power someone can have.

Builder: Then I thank you for the compliment.

Senator: When have your times been tough?

Builder: They've always been tough. They're tough today. And I'm independent. I depend on no one. And no one manipulates me.

Director: It seems likely you'd know when you depend on someone. But how would you know when you're being manipulated?

Builder: It's not easy, depending on the puppeteer's skill.

Director: Is it easier to know you've been manipulated, manipulated in the past?

Builder: That, too, can be hard.

Senator: Why?

Builder: Because you can be manipulated into doing something you want. And then you might not suspect.

Director: So how do you know?

Builder: You have to accept that you might never know.

Senator: There's really nothing you can do?

Builder: To know? No. But you can do things to cut your strings.

Director: What things?

Builder: You act a little crazy. You zigzag. You make yourself unpredictable.

Director: That's how you are at the helm of your great ship?

Builder: Yes, and I love it.

Senator: So you'd want to be a little crazy, unpredictable, even if you had no fear of manipulation?

Builder: I would. But, as it is, acting that way serves a purpose.

Director: What's the purpose of steering your ship?

Builder: Ruling my empire? It's good for its own sake.

Director: So you want to rule even when the going is rough?

Builder: Of course I do.

Director: When you have trouble, and you have to rethink your plans, your course, and you have to take pains over this—you're still doing what you want?

Builder: In an overarching sense? Yes.

Director: You see, Senator, that's the trick. That overarching sense.

Senator: Tell us more about it.

Director: Well, it's fairly simple. You choose an end, and you decide deep within that you'll always serve that end. Serving the end is what you want—no matter what it means.

Builder: See? Director understands.

Senator: But then it doesn't matter if someone manipulates you so long as you serve your end. As long as you stay on target, you're good.

Director: Is that how it is for you?

Senator: I serve the people. That's my end. And if I know in my heart I put them first, manipulated or not, I'm free.

Builder: How noble and just and right. And you, Director?

Director: I'm wondering.

Builder: About what?

Director: Manipulation. A true master manipulates you without your knowing.

Builder: That's why you need to be a little crazy, as I've said.

Director: But does that craziness really help?

Builder: Why wouldn't it?

Director: Because you can always be counted on to serve your end. That makes you predictable.

Builder: Well....

Director: What's your end, Builder?

Builder: You know what it is. My empire. Building it and keeping it strong.

Director: What if someone were to fool you into thinking a certain course of action would help build it up and keep it strong, but it wouldn't?

Builder: I wouldn't be fooled.

Director: Not even by someone supremely sly?

Builder: No.

Senator: And that's exactly why you can be fooled. That stubborn belief.

Builder: Yes, but that belief plays an important part.

Director: In what?

Builder: Keeping me from paranoia.

Senator: I would have thought you'd rather be paranoid than fooled.

Builder: How little you know.

— Trying

Director: Manipulation, paranoia—all such things aside, what counts is being able to judge when we're on course. No?

Builder: Exactly. Without that, nothing else matters.

Director: And if we stay on course over time?

Builder: That's the best we can hope. That's when we have success.

Senator: What if the course we chose leads to something bad?

Builder: Better the bad of our choosing.

Senator: That's easy to say. But I question your sense of success.

Builder: What's success to you?

Senator: Those who try, really try—no matter where they arrive—they have success.

Builder: Try, try, and try again? But at a certain point in trying, you have to wonder if you're a fool.

Director: How many times should we try? Once? Twice? Three times? How do we know when enough is enough? Senator, how many times would you try?

Senator: For a lofty goal? I'd never give up.

Builder: I'd give up if I stopped having fun. But, then again, my goals aren't lofty.

Director: Do you always have fun with your less than lofty goals?

Builder: Do you always have fun?

Director: Not always, no. But I don't give up.

Builder: Tell me about a time when you did give up.

Director: I tried to be a musician one summer. I tried and tried and tried.

Builder: And you didn't have any fun.

Director: No, I did have fun.

Builder: Then why did you give up?

Director: Would you believe me if I told you I was compelled to move on to more serious things?

Builder: What things?

Director: Words. As you seem to think, I'm good with them.

Builder: Then use your words and give us a definition of fun.

Director: How's this? Power and fun are one.

Builder: Ha, ha. I like your definition. It even rhymes. You do have a way with words.

Senator: But let's not joke about something like this.

Builder: Then you give us a definition of fun.

Senator: Fun is light hearted play.

Director: Ah, there! You see, Builder? Senator knows a thing or two. And I know the exercise of power isn't always light hearted play.

Builder: Isn't always? Ha, ha. It's never light hearted play.

Director: So if you're always taken with power, you never have any fun?

Builder: Haven't you heard of serious fun?

Director: I've heard people talk about it. But I thought they just meant they were having lots of fun.

Builder: No, it's something more.

Director: Then I think we should say fun is enjoyment.

Senator: Why?

Director: Because you can, for instance, enjoy a deep and intense game of chess. That's not light hearted. But you're having serious fun.

Builder: That's an excellent example.

Director: So how do you like your fun? Deep and intense, or superficial and.... What's the opposite of intense?

Builder: Mild.

Director: Mild. Really? Okay. So what'll it be? Deep and intense, or superficial and mild?

Builder: You know full well what it'll be.

Director: Deep and intense. After all, that's how empires are won.

— Some Fun

Builder: Why do I get the feeling you're poking fun?

Director: I don't know. Why would I poke fun at what comes of your intensity and depth? But let's consider what you've got. There are three basic things, as I see it. Money, workers, and buildings.

Builder: Yes, and most people would kill for what I have in those three.

Director: Most? I'm not sure about that. But some certainly would. Which of the three is most important to you?

Builder: They're equally important.

Director: You really wouldn't take the money over the others?

Builder: It wouldn't be an empire if I did.

Director: And that's what you really want. An empire.

Builder: Yes. Why, do you see something funny in that?

Senator: Builder, I don't see why you're becoming defensive.

Director: Yes, Builder. Why do you think I find something funny here?

Builder: You have a faint smile on your face when you say the word 'empire'.

Director: A faint smile?

Builder: It looks like you're amused.

Director: Well, I'm sorry. I'm not here to be amused. Or to poke fun.

Builder: What are you here for?

Director: Builder, you invited me. I wasn't sure why. Maybe you wanted to show off a worker to Senator, here? Make a sort of display?

Builder: You certainly seem amused to me now.

Senator: Oh, lighten up. So what if he's having some fun? You still have all the power here, don't you?

Director: Maybe we should change the subject.

Builder: To what?

Director: Loyalty.

Builder: What? Why should we talk about that?

Director: Your army of workers must be loyal, no?

Builder: Well, yes. Of course.

Director: How do you secure their loyalty?

Builder: Through paychecks.

Director: And?

Builder: The blacklist.

Director: How does the blacklist work?

Builder: Other employers fear reprisals from me if they hire someone against my wishes.

Director: So your workers are mercenaries who have little choice. And to be sure, by 'worker' we mean anyone who works for you at any level.

Builder: Yes, at any level—including outside consultants like you.

Director: You'd blacklist me? Make it so I can't find other work? You'd force me to break your power over me.

Builder: Good luck with that.

Director: Maybe Senator here could help.

Senator: I'd find you a job.

Director: You see, Builder? All your power is broken. That wasn't so hard.

Builder: No, it wasn't—assuming Senator stays employed.

Senator: You'd fund my opponent? That's just as well. I have a few more years before it comes to that. Plenty of time to find someone work.

Director: But, Builder, you must have known Senator has time. So what was your threat all about? Were you threatening bodily harm?

Builder: You can't work the senate from a hospital bed.

Director: If I didn't think you were kidding, I'd fear for our friend. But you're helping make our point.

Builder: What point?

Director: About the strength of the ox, how it's not power.

Builder: Unless it's properly used.

Director: And how is it properly used?

Builder: You have to have some finesse. After all, the power lies more in the art of the threat than in the force itself. Though you can't make empty threats.

Director: No, you can't. But that raises an interesting point. There are only so many threats you can make before they ring hollow.

Builder: Well, of course. Why is that interesting?

Director: Because we might be tempted to draw a certain conclusion. We might say the more good threats you can make, the more powerful you are.

Builder: I don't see how that's interesting, other than being true.

Senator: Why did you say it's tempting to draw that conclusion, Director?

Director: Because I'd see us draw another. The fewer the threats you have to make, the more powerful you are.

— Implied

Builder: That's because the threats are implied.

Senator: How so, implied?

Builder: It's always a threat if you know someone has power over you. The powerful one doesn't have to do a thing. The threat is implied.

Director: All power is a threat?

Builder: If it's power over you? Yes.

Director: Is it possible to have power but not have it over anyone?

Builder: I don't see the point.

Director: You could have power over yourself.

Builder: Yes, and I know we touched on this. But there's a danger.

Director: What danger?

Builder: That we'll sound like a self-help book! But let's be serious. What would it mean to have power over yourself? You can tell yourself what to do?

Senator: And then you do it, yes. There's no greater power than that in the world.

Builder: Sure, but how do you know what to tell yourself to do?

Senator: Well....

Builder: I'll tell you. It's implied by what we want.

Director: We have to match means to ends?

Builder: Means to our end, yes.

Director: So, in your case, the end is your empire.

Builder: Correct.

Director: And you judge your success by its size? In workers, buildings, and money?

Builder: I do.

Director: Remind us, Senator. What's your end?

Senator: The good of the people.

Builder: Noble. Ha, ha. And what about you, Director? What is it? Encouraging thought?

Director: I'm not sure I serve just one.

Builder: Pick one and work with us, here.

Director: I serve the cause.

Builder: What cause?

Director: Philosophy.

Builder: And what's the cause of philosophy?

Director: Do you mean what causes philosophy, or do you mean philosophy's cause, as in the cause philosophy serves?

Builder: You're a funny one. I want to know what you serve, what you're all about.

Senator: So he can get a handle on you, and manipulate you once he has. But philosophy doesn't let anyone do that, does it? Philosophy never gives its power away.

Director: It almost never does.

Builder: Almost?

Director: Sometimes it's tempted by love.

Builder: And if you give yourself away for love, what's left?

Director: Everything or nothing. I'm not sure.

Builder: Everything or nothing. Bah. You like to be a cipher, don't you?

Director: A writing in code? No, I wouldn't say that.

Builder: What would you say?

Director: That those who write themselves in cryptic words amount to nothing or less.

Senator: Clearly that's not you.

Builder: But answer the direct question. Do you write yourself in code?

Director: No. I'm literal in what I say.

Senator: But ironic, too.

Director: Maybe I'm a little guilty of that.

Builder: And so am I. I like to imply my meaning, not state it in so many words.

Senator: Is that what irony is?

Builder: Oh, what do you care? The point is that I'm making a great exception tonight.

Director: You're saying things in so many words?

Builder: Yes.

Director: Why? You said you like to imply your meaning.

Builder: And what I like more is saying what's on my mind—to someone who understands.

— Mercy

Director: Understanding can be a mercy in the struggle of life.

Builder: True, but that's not what I'm looking for.

Senator: Why not?

Builder: The need for mercy is a weakness.

Senator: Oh, why be so tough? We all need a little mercy at times. Mercy smooths the way.

Builder: Yes, but we all know what happens to those who take the smooth and easy way.

Senator: You don't want mercy for yourself? Fine. But have some for others.

Builder: Nothing would be easier.

Senator: How do you figure?

Builder: Look at it this way. Let's say someone doesn't do their job. No problem. Have mercy on them. And if they fail again? Have mercy again. And again. How easy this would be—until your company fails.

Senator: You're saying discipline is hard.

Builder: And it is.

Senator: But what if you enjoy the discipline? What if you're cruel?

Builder: Sometimes cruelty is all that makes discipline tolerable. But then it might go full circle.

Senator: What do you mean?

Builder: A struggling employee isn't doing anyone any good—especially themselves. Firing them is a mercy. Wouldn't you agree, Director?

Director: Cruel to be kind? Putting them out of their misery? And any sayings like this?

Builder: You make it sound like it's such a common thing.

Director: To base our thoughts on wise old sayings is a very common thing. But I don't expect the common from you.

Builder: Do you think it's easy to be cruel? That's why people need those sayings—to give them courage.

Senator: What's hard about cruelty?

Director: I think I might know. It's hard to be cruel when your nature is kind.

Senator: Then why not go on being kind?

Director: Builder gave us one idea. Your company might fail if you don't harden your heart.

Senator: But that's just the thing! Builder's heart is hard! It's nothing but. So firing someone, or whatever, isn't hard for him at all. He takes pleasure in the act!

Director: Is that true, Builder? Do you take pleasure in being cruel?

Builder: Honestly here with honest men? Yes.

Senator: Do you ever take pleasure in mercy?

Builder: Never. It's how I'm made.

Senator: Then let them break the mold after you.

Builder: Ha, ha. Yes, I like to think of myself as unique.

Director: Oh, but there are plenty of petty tyrants who take pleasure in being cruel.

Builder: True. But I'm not petty.

Director: You prefer cruelty on a grander scale?

Builder: Yes. And that's why I'd be good—as commander in chief.

— Kites

Senator: Ha! You want real armies, not just worker armies?

Builder: Real armies would be a delight.

Senator: I'm not sure how many would call killing machines a delight.

Builder: More reason the power belongs with me.

Director: Because you don't take it all that seriously?

Builder: Do you take seriously the things in which you delight?

Director: I delight in flying kites. Do I take the kites seriously? No, I don't. But I enjoy them nonetheless. And I think they enjoy it, too. Because, after all, kites are meant to soar.

Builder: And armies are meant to conquer.

Senator: Oh, that wasn't his point. Kites don't kill. Kites don't harm a thing. Director is talking about innocent pleasure.

Director: I am.

Builder: But let's substitute people for kites, which is what I think Director means. Isn't he a hypocrite?

Director: Why would I be?

Builder: You send your kites high, while you keep your feet firmly on the ground.

Director: I do keep them firmly on the ground. I walk everywhere I go.

Builder: You walk while they fly.

Senator: Builder, I don't understand. You make it sound like flying is something bad.

Builder: Only fools fly. And Director knows it.

Director: I don't know, Builder. I might fly if I could. But as things stand I can't.

Builder: Why can't you fly?

Director: Because I don't have wings.

Builder: I wouldn't be so sure.

Director: Trust me, Builder. I don't. I couldn't fly if my life depended on it. But if I find someone who can, and who wants to....

Builder: What? What then?

Director: I'd encourage them. I'd lend support. I'd help them do what they want. Do you see anything wrong with that?

Builder: No one encouraged me. I encouraged myself.

Director: I see.

Builder: What do you see?

Director: You've really been isolated all these years.

Builder: And what's so bad about that?

Director: Nothing—if you want what isolation brings.

Builder: And what do you think it brings?

Director: More often than not? Madness, but sometimes peace.

Builder: Do you think I'm mad?

Director: Well, I know you haven't found peace.

Builder: How do you know?

Director: Because you're fighting a full scale war.

Builder: How do you know I don't find peace in the fight?

Director: You don't show the signs.

Builder: And who shows these signs? You?

Director: I find peace in the fight. But, then again, my fight isn't yours.

Builder: What's your fight?

Director: One on the grandest possible scale.

Builder: I'm sure. But for what?

Director: I'll tell you part of it now. I fight to secure...

Builder: Secure what?

Director: ...for others...

Builder: Go on.

Director: ...an all too fleeting break...

Builder: Oh, get it over with!

Director: ...in the fight.

— The Fight

Builder: That's your grand scale? I don't even know what that is.

Director: You don't think we need a break when we fight?

Builder: We? Who is we? It's best to fight on your own. Don't you know that? But what's this fight?

Director: We each have our own. And when there's a break, we can focus more clearly on what that fight is. That's what we're doing here tonight.

Builder: You're helping me see?

Director: Yes, and tomorrow you're back in the ring.

Builder: Fair enough. So what do I need to see?

Director: You're not ready to hear it in so many words. But let me ask you this. Are you ever tempted to quit the fight?

Builder: Never.

Director: The ring is where you feel most alive?

Builder: Yes. Is it that way with you?

Director: Fighting my fight? I feel alive, yes. But I also feel alive with friends.

Senator: When do you not feel alive?

Director: I never feel dead.

Builder: Yes, but when do you feel most alive? In the fight or with friends?

Director: Alive is alive, Builder.

Builder: Then tell me something about your fight.

Director: I would have thought you'd like to know about my friends. But I'll tell you this. When I fight, I hold close the memories of my friends.

Builder: Why?

Senator: Oh, Builder. They encourage him.

Builder: I have memories that encourage me. But I also have something that makes me feel most alive.

Director: What is it?

Builder: Victory.

Director: Yes, victory is good.

Builder: Good? Victory is great! The greatest possible thing.

— Fighting

Senator: Director, I'm not clear on your fight. Can you say more?

Director: In the broadest possible sense, I fight against mistaken beliefs.

Senator: Why?

Director: Because I like to see people reclaim who they are.

Builder: That's the most interesting thing you've said tonight. But I'm afraid it's nonsense. Who would undertake this reclamation with you?

Director: Someone who wants to be whole.

Builder: And if they become whole?

Director: Sometimes? They take up the fight.

Builder: Your fight.

Director: Our fight.

Builder: But they fight this fight alone.

Director: With others who might become whole.

Builder: What does it mean to be whole?

Director: To be fully alive.

Builder: And that's the fight? Life?

Director: What better fight could there be?

Builder: I don't know. But let's be sure about this. You're saying mistaken beliefs can kill?

Director: Not 'can'—do. And when they don't completely kill, they deaden a part.

Builder: But who cares if people have mistaken beliefs that render them all but dead? It's easier to manipulate them when they do.

Director: Do you want them to have mistaken beliefs about... you?

Builder: If it helps me win my fight? Of course! All's fair in war, and whatever else.

Senator: Whatever else like love?

Builder: Sure, like love.

Senator: Funny how you put war first and obscured the love.

Builder: Funny how you don't understand there's no love without victory in war.

Senator: You have a false belief that war must come first.

Builder: You'd cure me of my false belief? Are you calling me less than fully alive?

Senator: Without love, we're less than we can be. Director, don't you agree?

Director: I do.

Senator: So we need to put love first.

Builder: Tell me, Senator. Does love just happen?

Senator: What do you mean?

Builder: Does love need no support? Can it just happen on its own?

Senator: I don't see what you're getting at.

Builder: I'm getting at this. We have to fight to secure our love.

Senator: If we can't fight, we can't have love?

Builder: Precisely.

Senator: But you either love or you don't. What does security have to do with it?

Director: Builder, maybe we should ask you what you love that you'd secure.

Builder: I love my empire.

Director: More than human beings?

Builder: Human beings are unreliable. To love them is folly. But my empire, on the other hand....

Director: Your empire is wholly within your control.

Builder: Yes, that puts it well.

Senator: So you love control. Which means you're capable of loving slaves. You have control over them.

Builder: Honestly? You're perfectly right. I control armies of slaves. And I love those slaves.

Director: So long as they serve your power. I wonder what beliefs they have.

Builder: I don't give that any thought. I just rely on fear and reward to keep them in line.

Senator: They believe in your power.

Builder: They don't believe in my power—they know it.

Senator: What if someone could make them question what they know?

Builder: To what end?

Senator: To show the slaves you have no power at all.

Builder: Ha, ha. Whoever shows them that will conquer—me.

— The Greatest Threat

Director: Short of that, someone can simply offer your workers other jobs.

Builder: But who will offer them jobs? I have the industry all locked up.

Director: Well, we need what we can call an outside force.

Builder: What outside force?

Director: An employer outside your reach.

Builder: My reach is long, you know.

Director: But maybe not long enough.

Builder: What have you got in mind?

Director: A rival power.

Builder: I wouldn't let one survive.

Director: But let's say one grows up, out of your sight. And one day you discover a very real threat.

Builder: I'm not that blind.

Director: Yes, but you can't be everywhere at once.

Builder: That's why I have my slaves.

Director: But what if they turn a blind eye to this threat, out of hatred for you? You agree that's possible, don't you?

Builder: Maybe.

Director: And then one day the threat is a fully fledged fact.

Builder: And, what, they'll hire away all my slaves? No chance.

Director: But your slaves will now have some hope. Hope opposes fear.

Builder: Then I'll train my guns on the new found threat.

Director: You'll go to war.

Builder: Of course. I've done it before, and I'll do it again.

Director: And what about love?

Builder: What about it?

Director: Does it play a role in your fight?

Builder: No more than it plays in yours.

Director: Oh, but it does play a role in mine.

Builder: How so?

Director: Love is what makes me fight.

Builder: Love for the one with false belief?

Director: Yes. If there's no love, I don't fight.

Builder: How convenient.

Director: There are too many people in the world for me to fight for them all.

Builder: And so you let love set your course.

Director: Do you know of a better way?

Builder: I do. You have to find and fight the biggest threat.

Director: That's what I do, in a way.

Builder: What way?

Director: I love those who pose the greatest threat. And I try to help turn them around.

Builder: The greatest threat to what? Themselves? That's a dangerous business, you know. What happens if they don't turn themselves around?

Director: They turn on me.

— Love 2

Builder: So how do you propose I introduce love to my fight?

Director: Find love, then fight for it.

Builder: It's all that simple?

Director: Yes. So what's your love?

Builder: I love.... Oh, this is stupid.

Director: Why?

Senator: I know why. It's because he's never loved a human being.

Director: Builder, is that true?

Builder: I'll tell you what's true. Love is a game.

Senator: How is it a game? We feel love and we love.

Builder: Yes, but what happens next? You love and then... what?

Director: Builder, you really don't know what happens next?

Senator: I'll say what happens next. You want to be with the one you love. And so you find ways to make that happen.

Builder: And if you can't?

Senator: Then I'd feel sorry for... you.

Builder: Ha! You, a politician, would feel sorry for me, the definition of success?

Senator: If you don't have love, what's your success worth?

Builder: Many billions of dollars. That's what it's worth.

Senator: Can all that money buy you love?

Builder: Oh, let's not start with tired old thoughts. The answer is yes.

Director: Builder, what's more important—love for people or things?

Builder: Most people are things.

Director: Yes, but really now. What do you think?

Builder: Love is meant for people.

Director: So who do you love?

Builder: Who do you love?

Director: I love you and Senator, too.

Builder: You don't really mean it.

Director: But I do.

Builder: What makes you love us?

Director: I love Senator because he's willing to try.

Builder: And me?

Director: Because of your potential.

Builder: Potential? As in I'm not living up to it now?

Director: Yes.

Builder: You really have some nerve.

Director: I do. And that helps me fight for what I love.

— Potential

Builder: So tell me about my potential.

Director: You might serve the cause.

Builder: Philosophy? Ha, ha.

Director: Why do you laugh?

Builder: Any fool can serve that cause.

Director: I don't think that's true.

Builder: Look, no offense. But other than you, I've never met a philosopher who wasn't playing silly games.

Director: What makes you think I'm not?

Builder: Never mind that. Tell me more about my potential.

Director: You have the potential to make a stand for love. There. Are you sure I'm not playing games?

Builder: I don't believe you are. So what gets in the way of my making that stand?

Director: Maybe you've been burned before?

Builder: And if I have?

Director: You need to learn to love again.

Builder: And you can teach me?

Director: I can help.

Builder: How?

Director: By getting you to open up and love me as a friend.

Builder: Senator, what do you think of all this?

Senator: Director has a point. You need to open up to someone, someone you can love.

Builder: And if I do?

Senator: The ice will thaw and you'll become whole.

Builder: And my empire?

Senator: You can't keep it the way you do now.

Builder: How will I keep it?

Senator: Your power will be love, not fear.

Builder: And what about the mercenaries who couldn't care less about love?

Senator: Let them go fight for someone else.

Builder: And if those who remain can't compete?

Senator: Train them harder in all your fighting ways.

Builder: Do you really think they'll fight from love?

Director: Yes, love—and interest, too.

Builder: But not everyone knows their interest.

Director: Then maybe you can help them here.

— Interest

Builder: And if I tell them the truth about their interest and they can't handle it?

Senator: Who can't handle their interest?

Builder: You might be surprised.

Senator: Those who love can always handle the truth.

Builder: I don't believe it.

Senator: Haven't you heard of the power of love?

Builder: That power is not what it seems.

Director: How does it seem?

Builder: It seems love gives you power, when in fact it takes your power away.

Director: You give your power to the one you love?

Builder: Yes, and you open yourself to manipulation.

Senator: How sad that's what you think. You need to find a kindred soul.

Builder: And if my soul is black?

Senator: Then there's no love for you.

Builder: But what about another blackened soul?

Director: Never mind that. You have some light in you.

Builder: So I can have love?

Director: It's possible, yes. And I think it's in your interest.

Builder: But why would I love someone who loves me?

Senator: Are you being serious?

Builder: Never more so.

Senator: You don't believe you're worth loving? So if someone loves you, they can't be worth loving in turn?

Builder: I have my doubts.

Director: If I love you, Builder, I'm not worth loving in turn?

Builder: With you it's not a question of worth. It's a matter of interest.

Senator: It's not in your interest to love this man back? Why?

Builder: Because he knows me too well.

— Knowledge 2

Director: And knowledge is power. But I'd let you know me at least as much as I know you.

Builder: But what's there to know? You go around asking questions with nothing to show.

Director: Ah, you mean if I were rich, you'd feel free to give me your love.

Builder: No, you know that's not the point.

Director: What is the point?

Builder: I have an empire to lose. You have... nothing.

Director: And knowledge of nothing is no power at all?

Builder: Yes.

Senator: But Director has a great deal to lose. His integrity.

Builder: Just what I don't have.

Director: Why do you sell yourself short?

Builder: You think you know me better than I know myself?

Director: Maybe.

Builder: So tell me what you know.

Director: You have an internal consistency.

Builder: Go on.

Director: You despise those who don't have your drive.

Builder: My drive is pure, yes.

Director: Your drive is for the empire you've built.

Builder: And tell me why that's what I've built.

Director: Because it's the one unambiguous thing in your life. And you worship it.

Builder: This man is smarter than I thought.

Senator: Then listen to him.

Builder: So, Director, tell me what's unambiguous in your life.

Director: My love.

Builder: You know what you love no matter what?

Director: I know what I love no matter what.

Senator: And that's because you have reasons for your love?

Director: But that's the thing. Do we need reason to love, or do we just love?

Builder: Say more.

Director: When we love, we find our reasons after the fact.

Builder: They're really not reasons?

Director: No, they are. And even more so.

Builder: How more so?

Director: They're tested by the fire of love—and come out clean.

Builder: Clean reasons. Yes, you're making some sense.

Senator: But I don't understand. Don't we have to have reason in order to love? I love someone because they're brave. That's my reason to love. I don't love them and then discover they're brave. That doesn't seem right.

Builder: No matter how it seems, it's true. Haven't you heard of love at first sight?

Senator: Of course I have. And now... you've posed a problem for me.

Builder: Say more.

Senator: My dear, departed wife—I loved her at first sight. And it was a love to last.

Builder: In that first glance, you saw all her qualities at once.

Senator: Yes, and no. I learned more as we got to know one another.

Builder: But what you learned was just an expansion on that first glance. No?

Senator: I suppose you have a point.

Builder: No doubt I do. And I would say that's a great power you had, all in that strike of the eye.

Director: Power is being able to see? What about manipulation and so on?

Builder: Everything follows from sight.

Director: Then what does it take to see?

Builder: An openness. A willingness to trust your eyes.

Senator: I think it takes knowledge. If I look at computer code, for instance, with no knowledge of the language, I won't see a thing. It will mean nothing to me. But if I know the language....

Builder: You have a point. It takes knowledge in order to see, knowledge of the various human ways.

Senator: Yes, Builder. But once you see, will you do what it takes—to say what you saw?

— Saying

Builder: Why say anything at all?

Senator: Because otherwise you can't be sure.

Builder: Sure of what?

Senator: What you think you saw.

Builder: Really? And when you say what you think you saw, what happens then?

Senator: You get affirmation from others.

Builder: What if I'm the only one who sees?

Senator: Well, that's a problem.

Builder: Why? Can't I just act on my vision?

Senator: To your benefit alone?

Builder: What's wrong with that? It's my vision, my knowledge.

Director: Yes, but I'd like to clarify something.

Builder: By all means.

Director: Senator, do you ever say what you saw in another, to that other?

Senator: I do, but with a great deal of tact.

Builder: You say it even if what you saw was bad?

Senator: Even then.

Builder: Why?

Senator: I might be a help.

Director: And if you see something good?

Senator: I love to share the good.

Builder: Yes, but let's get back to the bad, the ugly. You're really not sure of them until you speak?

Senator: Absent a blatant bad act? Yes. The way the person reacts tells me if I'm right.

Builder: But if they're bad, won't they be good at putting on an act? One that fools you?

Senator: Maybe. But in telling them what I see, I hope to prompt them to change, regardless of what they say in response.

Builder: Your hope will be nothing but that. No one will change from this. I've never seen it happen.

Senator: Maybe that's because you never tried.

Builder: I wasn't always the way I am now, you know.

Senator: So you tried?

Builder: I tried and tried and no one changed.

Director: Why do you think it didn't work?

Builder: Because people don't change. Oh, they can make an effort for a while, but they always go back.

Senator: So what should we do? Only show them the good, and keep the bad to ourselves?

Builder: Keep it all to yourself. You'll have less trouble that way.

Director: Builder, if we keep the bad to ourselves but share the good, what does that make us?

Builder: Good on the edges but corrupt to the core.

Senator: Corrupt? How so?

Builder: You see the bad and say nothing. If that's not corrupt, I don't know what is.

Senator: But what are you saying? You recommend we be corrupt?

Builder: Yes.

Senator: You just don't want anyone to point out the bad in you.

Builder: Why would it matter? I know the bad in me. And I make it known for all to see.

Director: And how's that working out?

Builder: Splendidly. Just look around.

Senator: But then your bad can't be that bad. Or you're not really making it known for all to see.

Builder: Why?

Senator: Because otherwise you wouldn't stand a chance.

Builder: Things wouldn't be so splendid? You sound like a realist, Senator. So I'll tell you the truth. My bad is there to see, for those with eyes to see.

Senator: Eyes to see? Who can't see you causing fear?

Builder: Oh, that's not the bad I mean.

Director: Who can see the bad you mean? Those with bad in themselves?

Builder: Yes, and I wonder about you.

Director: Me? What do you wonder?

Builder: You see the bad in me. You have the eyes. So what does that say about you?

Senator: It doesn't say anything. You don't have to be a bird to recognize one in flight.

Builder: And what sort of bird am I?

Senator: I'm not sure.

Builder: Well, no matter. I know what you mean. And that's why I fly—by night.

— Night

Director: Ah, the metaphorical night.

Builder: There's nothing metaphorical about the dark. It's very real.

Director: I'm sure it is. But why would you want to be in the dark?

Builder: Senator, is all of your legislative work done in the full light of day?

Senator: No.

Builder: Now, if even honest Senator here can't do everything in the light, how can I?

Director: Senator, why can't you do everything in the light of day?

Senator: Because I have to compromise.

Director: On your principles?

Senator: Well....

Director: Let me see if I understand. You tell the voters you believe x.

Senator: And I do believe x.

Director: But when you compromise with your peers, you sell x short?

Senator: No. I do the best for x I can.

Director: Why can't that best be in the light?

Senator: Because it's ugly to reveal what's traded for what.

Builder: You see? There's a human need to keep the ugly from light.

Senator: A human need? No, it's just a political fact.

Director: Builder, what ugliness do you deal in?

Builder: Power has its ugly side.

Director: How so? And what specifically? I would have thought true power could thrive in the light.

Builder: Why would you think that?

Director: Because it's the powerless that hide.

Builder: Look. Do you agree that power always involves manipulations?

Director: Always?

Builder: Oh, now isn't the time to be particular.

Director: Fine. Power involves manipulations.

Builder: Well, it's never wise to reveal those manipulations. Do you need to know why?

Director: I do.

Builder: It's because they're ugly.

Director: Really? I didn't think your imagination was so limited.

Builder: What are you talking about?

Director: Can't you think of beautiful manipulations?

Builder: Can you?

Director: I don't have to. Someone else has done the thinking for me.

Builder: I don't believe you let anyone do the thinking for you. But tell me what you mean.

Director: Think of the comic plays of the Bard. They're full of manipulations, manipulations we enjoy.

Builder: I saw a few of those plays a long time ago. Their manipulations generally have to do with love.

Director: And what better power to have than power over love?

Senator: But they're comedies. We know they're not true. We know there's no power over love.

Builder: You don't have enough faith in power.

Senator: And you don't have enough faith in love.

— Funny

Director: Which is more reliable? Power or love?

Builder: Reliable? That's a funny question.

Director: Then maybe you should give a funny answer.

Builder: Alright, I will. But we need to modify the question a bit.

Senator: How?

Builder: It's not a question of power itself. It's a question of love, love of power.

Senator: You had to steal love over to your side, didn't you?

Builder: Oh, wait until you hear the answer before you complain. And here it is. You'll never hear of a lover of power having an affair, cheating on their power. They're loyal and true when it comes to their love. They keep their faith.

Senator: Your answer would be funny if you didn't believe it.

Director: Tell us, Builder. What does it mean to love power?

Builder: Do you want another funny answer?

Director: Funny or not as long as it's true.

Builder: To love power is to know it for what it is.

Senator: To know it is to love it?

Builder: Yes, that way too.

Director: And what is it?

Builder: The most beautiful thing in the world.

Senator: I should have known you couldn't resist. Love is the most beautiful thing in the world.

Builder: Love is often a great big mess.

Senator: How so?

Builder: You know how so. But let me give you an example. Love compels you to make mushy declarations.

Senator: What's wrong with that?

Builder: They're unseemly and better not made.

Senator: Why are they unseemly?

Builder: Because they show you're weak.

Senator: Without power, you mean.

Builder: Yes, without power.

Senator: And maybe that's good.

Builder: Good to be powerless? Ha, ha.

Senator: Wouldn't that be a relief? To set down the burden of power through love?

Builder: Honestly? There's something to what you say. But it's much like putting down the burden of life—through death.

— Surrender

Senator: You're just afraid to be swept off your feet by love.

Builder: No, I simply won't trade my empire for love.

Senator: Why not?

Builder: What could someone possibly love in me more than what I've built? What would it mean if I'd throw it all away?

Senator: Sacrifice it for your love? I think someone would be greatly moved by that.

Builder: And then where does that leave me? Powerless and in love.

Senator: That sounds like a good place to be.

Builder: You'd trade your career for love?

Senator: Yes, but I didn't have to.

Builder: What about your love for the people? You would have traded that, too?

Senator: If I left office for love, I would have found ways to serve the people, just the same. But you can't let your empire go. You're completely attached. I was never that way with my career.

Builder: Director, what do you think?

Director: I don't see why you can't have both career and love.

Builder: What little free time I have, I'd have for my love?

Director: Right. As they say, it's not the amount of time—it's the quality.

Builder: What would make for high quality?

Senator: Surrendering yourself completely to love.

Builder: Let my power go for a time? But what if my love holds power over me? What if they don't let go the way that I let go? Am I to be a slave?

Senator: You need to find someone who lets go, too.

Builder: That takes a complete and mutual trust.

Senator: It does.

Builder: And you knew love like that?

Senator: I did.

Builder: But you've never had real power, not power like mine.

Senator: Power is power. Whether you have much or little, it's hard to let go.

— Letting Go

Builder: But this is foolish. What point is there in letting go?

Senator: Don't you want to experience love?

Builder: I have experienced love. Little good that it did.

Director: What was that little good?

Builder: Oh, it felt nice. But it was more a distraction than anything else.

Senator: If you describe love as nice, I can't believe it was truly love.

Builder: How much more true does it have to be? Do I have to suffer terrible longing? Who needs that? Did you?

Senator: Suffer terrible longing? No. But that's because I knew she loved me.

Builder: Knew? Well, if I find someone I know, absolutely know loves me—loves me for what I am, a great man of power—I might love in turn.

Senator: Yes, but you're not willing to take that first step, to take a chance. You're afraid you'll get hurt. Some man of power you turn out to be.

Builder: I don't want to waste my time.

Director: But if love feels nice....

Builder: Yes, if love feels nice then why not love? I'll tell you why. As I said, it's a distraction.

Director: Can't you use a distraction at times?

Builder: Well, you may have a point. But how many people out there view love as nice? I think it would be hard to find someone like that.

Senator: Someone interested in a part-time love? In an amusement for you?

Builder: And for them, too. Oh, don't be disgusted with me. I know my limits. That's the only love I could stand.

Director: You had a deeper love long ago.

Builder: How do you know what I had?

Director: You wear the scars.

Builder: What exactly do you mean?

Director: You lied about love. You felt the terrible longing.

Builder: And why would I lie about that?

Director: Because it shows you were powerless.

Senator: That's why you stay away from love. You fear for your power.

Builder: I'm glad you're enjoying this amateur psychology. Well, so what if I've sublimated my love?

Senator: Sublimated? You exchanged love for power.

Builder: And it was a very good trade. But tell me. What do you think it would cost me to buy back my love?

Senator: Everything you've got.

Builder: Then it's not a fair trade. I have more than almost anyone in the world. And love wants all that? Then love is a greedy –

Director: Best not say it.

Builder: Why?

Director: Because that's what you need to let go.

Senator: Your contempt for love.

Builder: What will letting go get me?

Senator: Peace.

Builder: Even if I don't have love?

Senator: Being open to love is half the fight.

Builder: Peace, a fight—which is it? And what's the other half?

Director: Finding ways to woo.

— Wooing

Builder: Ways to woo? And what's wooing to you?

Director: Ah, I thought you might need a primer. Wooing is gentle persuasion toward love.

Builder: Why do you think I don't know that? But I'll tell you this. You'll never win or manage an empire with gentle persuasion.

Senator: Let's not get distracted by your empire. Let's stick to love. Director, can you tell us why we need to persuade? After all, love is or it isn't.

Director: True, but the ways of love can be rough or smooth.

Builder: And smooth love is one big persuasion?

Director: Yes. And I'd say it's the same for empire.

Builder: What do you know about empire? Woo the people I rule? Wooing can't win their love.

Director: What can?

Builder: Foolishness. Generous seeming actions. Failure to be firm when you must.

Director: What about justice?

Builder: What is justice?

Senator: Getting what you deserve.

Builder: If a clear eyed ruler gives the people what they deserve, trust me—they won't like it.

Senator: Oh, you're being ridiculous. Not everyone deserves something bad.

Builder: Don't be so sure. But, Director, say more about keeping love smooth.

Director: What do you want me to say?

Builder: Anything.

Director: How's this? You have to live up to the love in your other's eyes.

Builder: So love makes you better than you were?

Director: What do you think?

Builder: That's too romantic for me. But tell me this. How do you find your love?

Senator: I'll answer that. You just do.

Builder: You stumble into it?

Senator: Honestly? That's what worked for me.

Builder: How about you, Director?

Director: I do my share of stumbling, but not when it comes to love.

Builder: What do you do?

Director: I set traps.

Builder: Ha, ha. What sort of traps?

Director: Essays on love.

Builder: Essays you wrote?

Director: No, essays I borrowed from others.

Builder: What do you do with them?

Director: I give them to friends.

Builder: And what do they do with them?

Director: They share them with anyone who seems fair.

Builder: Fair in the old sense? As in beautiful?

Director: Don't you think fair in the modern sense is beautiful, too?

Builder: You have a point. But, in either sense, you ask your friends to share the essays with beautiful seeming people?

Director: I do. And you're right to say 'seeming'. I have to prove they're beautiful. But I'm getting ahead of myself.

Builder: Yes, you are. So what happens when your friends share the essays on love?

Director: Sometimes they poach the trapped.

Builder: You mean the fair fall in love with them.

Director: Yes. But sometimes my friends deliver.

Builder: Let me guess. The fair one is intrigued by the essay, and by extension is intrigued by you.

Director: You see? The fair ones come to me.

Builder: And when they do?

Director: We talk about love.

Builder: That's how you test them on their beauty.

Director: That's right.

Builder: And if they're beautiful?

Director: Then we pass the time in a wonderful way.

— Pastime

Builder: So love is some sort of hobby for you?

Director: No. Love is my serious work.

Builder: Oh, stop teasing. Why don't you take it seriously?

Director: But I do. I'm very serious when I set my traps.

Builder: And you're serious when you test the beauty of those you trap?

Director: Very.

Builder: What's the first test?

Director: I ask them what they liked about the essay on love.

Builder: What's a wrong answer they give?

Director: A wrong answer? Well, it's... it's....

Builder: There is no wrong answer, is there?

Director: You've caught me.

Builder: And the right answer? But I know the answer to this. Every answer is right.

Director: You've all but figured me out. So how does this sound to you?

Builder: What, you mean do I have time for this nonsense? Of course not.

Director: Not even if you write an essay on love?

Builder: Me? Ha!

Director: What's the matter?

Builder: Let's say I do. What am I supposed to do with the fair ones I catch?

Director: Talk to them and pass a pleasant afternoon.

Builder: I don't have afternoons to spare.

Director: Really? Not even for love?

Builder: You're not even talking about love. You're talking about some game.

Director: But what if I tell you I'm hoping I'll one day meet my One through this game?

Builder: You believe in that foolishness?

Senator: I found my One. And it wasn't foolish to me.

Builder: Yes, yes. But you're an exception.

Senator: Maybe you are, too.

Builder: If I meet my One, it'll be in the course of my empire's affairs.

Director: So you're just counting on luck. Is that how you run your business?

Builder: Of course not.

Director: And that's because your business is more important than love. You wouldn't entrust it to luck.

Builder: You sound like you should be running a dating service.

Director: I can get you dates. Is that what you want? No effort required on your part.

Builder: And what would make someone want to go on a date with me? Hmm?

Director: Maybe we shouldn't tell them who you are.

Builder: What would we tell them?

Director: That you're someone I met through work, which is true. But I'm afraid we'd have to lie about your name. And maybe have you wear a disguise.

Builder: Oh, this is ridiculous.

Director: You're not even willing to try it just once?

Builder: This would be someone you know?

Director: Yes.

Builder: Do you already have someone in mind?

Director: I do.

Builder: What's she like?

Director: She? You'll just have to see.

Builder: Why not tell me about her now?

Director: First, I don't want to ruin the surprise. Second, I don't want to prejudice you.

Builder: I only have to commit to one afternoon?

Director: Yes. Why not make it a late lunch and see where things go?

Builder: I don't like being set up like this.

Director: You don't want to feel you owe me something if things go well?

Builder: I have no problem owing. But I don't know how I could pay you back. And I need to know that before I owe.

Director: You don't want any vague debts hanging over your head.

Builder: That's right. I need to know where I stand, and how I can get back to even.

Director: What if you help me with one of my traps?

Builder: An essay on love? You want me to show it around?

Director: Throughout your empire, yes.

Builder: What, send it attached to a message for all to see?

Director: Why not?

Builder: They'll think I've gone mad!

— Madness

Director: But this is how you prove you haven't gone mad.

Builder: Because the essay shows I care about love, and it's madness not to care about love?

Director: Yes. The essay is a start.

Builder: See? I knew you couldn't leave this as a one time transaction. You want it to be a beginning.

Director: Don't you? Or would you rather be perceived as mad? And if you're perceived as mad...

Builder: Finish the thought.

Director: ...it might drive you mad.

Builder: And you think I'm the one who uses fear to persuade! So if I know the two of you think I'm mad, that knowledge might worm its way around in my brain and make me mad?

Director: It depends on how much respect you have for us.

Builder: If someone you admire says you're crazy, eventually you'll go crazy? Do you know what nonsense that is?

Director: Why is it nonsense? If someone I admire above all others tells me I'm mad, I might wonder if I'm mad. And if I start to wonder if I'm mad, I might come to think I'm mad. And isn't that the first step in going mad?

Builder: That never happens when you're tough minded.

Director: Maybe you've never admired someone highly enough. Have you?

Builder: I admire myself.

Director: Then don't tell yourself you're crazy.

Builder: Why would I?

Director: Because you might come to see your empire has all been for nothing. Has it?

Builder: Of course not.

Director: What's it been for?

Builder: My pleasure.

Director: What pleasure is that?

Builder: The sort that comes from great power.

Director: Power is pleasure?

Builder: The greatest pleasure there is.

Director: But if power is pleasure, is pleasure power?

Builder: Count on you to take that crazy turn.

Director: Is it so crazy?

Builder: Of course it is.

Director: Why?

Builder: Because I take pleasure in a hot shower each day. That shower isn't power.

Senator: Say that to someone living in a poor land stricken with drought.

Builder: Yes, yes. But even in such a land people can laugh. And they take pleasure in that. Does that make laughter power?

Director: I think there's a power in laughter.

Builder: Of course you do. What is that power?

Director: It's power over fear.

Builder: Now you've said something interesting. Say more.

Director: I'll certainly say more. I'm at your command.

Senator: I'll say it. Laughter banishes fear, if only for a moment. It's a great relief.

Director: Isn't power over fear one of the greatest powers there can be?

Builder: You have a point.

Director: Yes, but there's one more point to make.

Builder: Oh?

Director: There are different types of laughter. There's fear-conquering laughter—and then there's the laughter of the mad.

— Laughter

Builder: Describe the laughter of the mad.

Director: It's any laughter that doesn't leave you free from fear.

Builder: Then no one ever was fully sane.

Director: Senator, do you mix laughter with fear?

Senator: I admit I'm not perfect here. But you, Director? I haven't heard you laugh that way tonight. Do you ever?

Director: I don't.

Builder: Why not?

Director: I'm terribly afraid of going mad.

Builder: Ha! Fear steadies your nerves?

Director: Fear teaches me to bite my tongue.

Builder: We usually bite our tongues when we would speak.

Director: Isn't laughter speech?

Builder: So what do you do? Speak laughter inside?

Director: Mad within and sane without? If I am that way, why would I say? But this talk of laughter has me wondering. What does it have to do with power and love?

Builder: Laughter and power? There's nothing funny about power.

Director: No, not that we can say. But what about love?

Builder: You want my honest opinion?

Director: I expect nothing less of you.

Builder: There's nothing funny in love.

Director: Why not?

Builder: You really want me to say?

Director: I really want you to say.

Builder: I don't think you'll believe me.

Director: Try me.

Builder: There's nothing funny in love... because love is holy. Are you surprised?

Director: No. But are you saying you have no time for the holy?

Builder: It's not so much that. It's that I expect perfection in love.

Director: There's nothing funny about perfection.

Builder: No, nothing funny at all.

Director: But what if we could laugh at the quest for perfection?

Builder: Why would we?

Director: Because we know it's an impossible goal.

Builder: So we should laugh at the impossible?

Director: What else can we do? Show reverence for it?

Builder: I think we're on to something important here. What if I say I do have reverence for the impossible?

Director: I'd say you're a fool.

Builder: And then you'd laugh at me?

Director: Honestly? I don't know.

Builder: Why not?

Director: Because I'd feel sorry for you.

Builder: You've trapped me, it seems.

Director: How so?

Builder: Oh, you know how so.

Director: Then tell me so I can be sure.

Builder: I'm not in the habit of saying how I'm trapped.

Director: What is your habit?

Builder: To get away—however I can.

— Friendship

Senator: I only hope in getting away you don't sacrifice your friendship.

Builder: What friendship can I expect from a subordinate?

Director: You assume I'll keep working for you.

Builder: If you don't, you're on the special blacklist, you know.

Director: The special blacklist?

Senator: Don't abuse your power, Builder.

Builder: And how should I use it?

Senator: To build people up, not tear them down.

Builder: Build them up so they'll rebel against me?

Senator: Why do you assume your friends would rebel against you?

Builder: Asks someone with no real power, someone at the mercy of votes.

Director: So how is it?

Builder: How is what?

Director: Are friends beyond the limit of power?

Builder: I'm not sure what you mean.

Director: I mean, if you have real power, you can't have friends?

Builder: You're the one who spoke of isolation.

Director: Yes, and the madness it brings.

Builder: With friends I won't go mad?

Director: Friends can stop you from going off the rails.

Builder: Ha, ha. You use that tired metaphor of tracks. Who says I want to stay on track?

Director: If you don't, where will you go?

Builder: Wherever I please.

Director: And you can't do that with friends?

Builder: Tell me, Director. What's a friend?

Director: Someone you enjoy spending time with.

Builder: And that's all?

Director: Well, no, I could say friends are loyal to friends. They help each other when they can.

Builder: What if I don't need the help?

Senator: We all need help, Builder.

Builder: And the more help given the better the friend? Well then, you two must feel very good about yourselves—given how desperate for help I am.

— Voids

Senator: Please don't be sarcastic.

Builder: Does sarcasm bother you?

Senator: Of course it does.

Builder: Why?

Senator: Because sarcasm is a pathetic attempt to wound.

Builder: Why pathetic?

Senator: Because the strong are never sarcastic.

Builder: What are they?

Senator: Ironic.

Builder: Irony isn't sarcasm?

Senator: Of course it's not. In fact, I'd say sarcasm is irony without the strength.

Builder: So when you say you can't tell if I'm being sarcastic, you're really saying you wonder how strong I am.

Senator: That's a fair way to put it, yes.

Builder: Then watch me dry up your party's funds, and see what you think.

Senator: Honestly? I couldn't care less if you dry them up. And that's my strength.

Builder: Okay, Senator. So tell me why we should be friends.

Senator: It doesn't work like that. It's not why we should. It's why we are.

Builder: Are we friends?

Senator: Aren't we?

Builder: How can we make our friendship more clear?

Senator: We can refuse to let power get in the way.

Builder: Get in the way? But power is what I am. Director, what do you think I'd be if I set my power aside?

Director: Maybe you'd be the clothes you wear.

Builder: But be serious.

Director: You'd be the people you love.

Builder: So I'd have to make a leap.

Director: Can you say more?

Builder: I'd have to leap from loving power to... love.

Senator: Exactly.

Builder: But what if I'm not loved in turn?

Senator: That's the most honest thing you've asked tonight.

Builder: What's the answer?

Senator: You'd go a while without power or love, until you find the latter.

Builder: And then I go back to power?

Senator: And then you go back.

Builder: What's it like without power or love, Director?

Director: You think I'd know? I can guess what it would be like for you. You'd feel a great void.

Builder: Why would I ever do anything that results in a void?

Director: Isn't your chase after power the result of a void?

Builder: If it is, doesn't it make sense to fill that void up? But what about you? Do you have a void?

Director: I do. And I fill it with friendship and love.

Builder: I don't believe you.

Senator: What would you have him fill it with?

Builder: What can he fill it with? Power. But what would I have him fill it with? I'd have him try anything else.

Senator: Because you don't want the competition.

Builder: There's only so much power to go round. Or do you think we can share?

Director: We can certainly share friendship.

Builder: And love?

Director: Love of friends? Sure.

Builder: But what about love love?

Director: Love love? Romantic love?

Builder: Oh, why does it have to be romantic? Love, and you know what I mean.

Director: You're asking if we can share the object of our love? It's possible, I suppose. But wouldn't we usually rather not?

— Alike

Builder: Usually rather not? Ha, ha. We never want to share. All of us are selfish here.

Director: So you agree?

Builder: With what?

Director: The notion that love has something in common with power.

Senator: Director, what do you mean?

Director: The quest for power is selfish, no?

Senator: It is.

Director: And what about the quest for love?

Senator: It's selfish in a way. But in a way it's not.

Director: What way is it not?

Senator: You share the love with your beloved.

Director: So the two aren't really alike?

Senator: Power and love? No, of course they're not.

Director: But let's be sure. Don't you think when you love someone they have power over you?

Senator: But if they love you, too, you have power over them. The powers cancel each other.

Director: And that's what sharing is?

Senator: Sharing is when the powers reinforce one another, too.

Builder: Cancel and reinforce? That's impossible.

Senator: Love makes the impossible possible.

Builder: So does false belief. But there's a basic problem here. Power is never perfectly matched. So there can be no cancellation.

Director: But can't powers can be matched closely enough to think of them as equal?

Builder: I suppose. But that equality is still a fiction.

Director: Tell us. Do you ever watch the fights?

Builder: I do. Why do you ask?

Director: Haven't you ever seen two fighters who seem perfectly matched?

Builder: Of course. And those are the best fights to watch. But, Director, someone always wins.

Director: Well, what if the fight went on no end?

Builder: You're really equating love with a fight?

Director: Oh, maybe the example was poor. But my point is this. Can't two lovers be so well matched that things are always interesting?

Builder: That's rare, you know.

Senator: Someone seeking the perfect shouldn't mind the rare.

Builder: Yes, but I've already admitted I've sublimated my love. And look at the result. One of the greatest empires of modern times. So you tell me. Who can match that?

Director: Let's go to the fights again. Haven't you noticed that fighters tend to fight best when fighting their strongest foe?

Builder: I have.

Director: Couldn't it be the same with love?

Builder: Great power in love brings out the other's power, too?

Senator: Of course it does! This is truly a beginner's course in love.

Builder: And you're such an expert? Oh, I'm sorry, my friend. I forgot about your wife.

Senator: She still makes me strong, you know.

Director: That's obvious to anyone with eyes to see. So if we're at our best, it's likely we've been reinforced.

Builder: We can say that.

Director: But you don't believe it.

Builder: I'm at my best when I fight a strong foe—in business. But shouldn't love be a break from the fight?

— Belief

Director: Senator, do we rest in love, or do we have to exercise our strength?

Senator: Both.

Builder: Here we are with impossibilities again.

Senator: We take a break from the world, and exercise muscles of the soul.

Builder: Muscles of the soul? Do you really believe in the soul? As in more than a figure of speech?

Senator: The soul is the seat of love. Of course I believe in it.

Builder: So if I don't believe in the soul, I can't love?

Senator: Love might prove to you you have a soul.

Builder: So I can love without believing in soul. Director?

Director: You can love without belief. But love might make you believe, as Senator says.

Builder: How can I stop it from making me believe?

Senator: Why would you want to do that?

Builder: Because beliefs interfere with power. Beliefs allow you to rest, to go to sleep.

Senator: And you never sleep.

Builder: Not when I can help it. And certainly not from belief.

Director: Builder, I'm wondering something. When you say belief interferes with power, are you talking about political power?

Builder: No, I'm talking about real power. Power beyond politics.

Director: What's beyond politics? Religion?

Builder: No, religion is politics in a different form.

Director: So what's beyond?

Builder: Pure power. The power of no belief.

Senator: The power of tyranny, you mean.

Builder: Tyrants have always been treated unfairly.

Director: How so?

Builder: They do much good. They come to power in turbulent times and stabilize things.

Senator: Stabilize things through fear.

Builder: Yes, through fear.

Director: But when they come to power, that's a political thing. Isn't it?

Builder: Tyrants suspend the political. That's the secret to their rule.

Senator: I thought fear was the secret.

Builder: Fear is never a secret to those who fear. Nor to those who make them fear.

Director: But how can you suspend the political?

Builder: By concentrating it all in yourself.

Director: So the tyrant never gets a moment's rest.

Builder: Never.

Director: Is that somehow justification?

Builder: Justification for the tyrant's rule? It is. The unceasing work of the tyrant allows the people rest.

Senator: And yet they fear.

— Fear

Director: Fear gives you no rest.

Builder: Yes, yes. But people always fear. It's in their nature. It's just a question of degree. A smaller amount of fear can feel like rest. Besides, under tyranny people don't have to bear the burden of rule.

Senator: The burden of rule? What burden is it to vote?

Builder: In order to vote well you have to keep up with events.

Senator: And that's what makes tyranny good? You don't have to keep up? You don't have to watch the news?

Builder: Keeping up with what's really going on is no small thing.

Senator: But how is it any better in a tyranny? You have to keep up with the tyrant's whims.

Builder: Well....

Senator: And the fear is certainly worse in a tyranny. Tyrants love to make people fear.

Builder: You don't think there are elected officials who love to make people fear?

Senator: It's nowhere near the same thing.

Director: You resist these officials, don't you?

Senator: Of course I do.

Builder: Then you'd better hope the democracy lasts—because your resistance in a tyranny would be crushed, if the tyrant is worth his salt.

Director: His? Didn't you say not to count out the women? Can't they be tyrants, too?

Builder: Yes, but it's less likely.

Director: Why?

Builder: They don't often have tyrannical drive.

Director: Really? But is that a compliment or an insult?

Builder: It is what it is.

Senator: I think they have the drive as often as men, but haven't always had the chance to rule.

Director: That may be. But let's save this topic for another time. What I want to know now is if tyrants fear.

Builder: Do they fear? Ha! Of course they fear! They fear being deposed.

Director: Do you have that fear?

Builder: I?

Senator: You're the one who said you fear to lose what you love.

Builder: There is a certain fear, yes.

Senator: So in tyranny everyone fears.

Builder: True. But the tyrant manages to be free from fear, at times.

Senator: What times?

Builder: When he makes others feel exceptional fear.

Director: Does the tyrant laugh at their exceptional fear?

Builder: Yes, he does. And laughter drives away fear.

Director: Do the subjects ever laugh at the tyrant?

Builder: No, I don't think they do.

Director: They're too afraid even to laugh?

Builder: They're weak.

Director: And if they were strong?

Builder: Tyrants do away with the strong.

Director: So the empire is weak?

Builder: No, the empire is strong.

Senator: I don't understand.

Builder: A body animated by a single competent will is strong. Divided bodies are weak.

Senator: But isn't a body stronger still if made up of the strong?

Builder: The strong won't put up with domination by the single competent will. They eventually rebel.

Director: So your officer corps, so to speak, is filled with... the weak?

Builder: Yes, in a sense. But if they give themselves over to me, if they trust in me completely—together they'll be strong.

Director: I didn't give myself over completely to you.

Builder: You weren't part of my officer corps.

Senator: Nor will he ever be.

Builder: Oh, why say that, Senator? Director, can't you see this happening one day?

Director: As I look into the mists of the future, I see no time when this might be.

Builder: You don't have to join the main corps. You could rise above.

Director: And do what?

Builder: Take direction directly from me. I'd make it worth your while.

Director: Money? I can get enough of that elsewhere.

Builder: Yes, but what about power?

Director: Power sharply limited by your power? No thanks.

Builder: Ha, ha! Do you see, Senator? Director wants unbridled power!

Senator: I think he just wants nothing to do with tyranny.

Builder: But you're tempted by tyranny, aren't you, Director?

Director: The only ones tempted don't know what it is.

Builder: And what is it?

Director: Above all else? Isolation. And, yes, you can surround yourself with sycophants, and the seemingly strong of your corps. But they leave you more isolated than ever. Don't you agree?

Builder: I agree. You have some insight into my state. Though I have to wonder how you gained such insight. Perhaps there's a touch of the tyrannical in you?

Director: Perhaps there is. And perhaps we all have a touch, brought out when circumstances are right. But what we do with it differs.

— Starving

Builder: Well, you know what I do with mine.

Director: You feed it and watch it grow.

Builder: And what do you do with yours? Starve it and let it die? But do we ever want to let part of us die?

Senator: If it's a bad part, sure. Let it die.

Builder: And you're sure tyranny is bad?

Senator: Nothing worse.

Director: Are we content to let it die in us, or do we want to bring on the death in others, too?

Senator: That's what I think philosophy is for, or should be if it's not.

Builder: Is that what philosophy does? It tries to put the greatest part of me to death?

Director: Philosophy tries to put everyone to death.

Builder: Everyone to death? You'd better explain.

Director: Have you heard of death and rebirth?

Builder: I have.

Director: Philosophy encourages rebirth. Don't you think being reborn is good?

Builder: I'm not exactly persuaded of that.

Director: Why not?

Builder: What do I get from rebirth?

Director: Your youth again, but at an older age. What could be wrong with that?

Builder: Youths aren't exactly wise.

Director: Ah, so it's wisdom you seek. What if you could be young and wise?

Builder: Wise beyond my years? That's the oldest lie there is.

Director: How so?

Builder: These young ones think they're wise but they're not. And, in truth, they're not even young.

Director: They're unwise and old before their time?

Builder: Yes.

Director: Why?

Builder: They haven't had enough experience to know. And yet they think they know.

Director: And others believe they know?

Builder: That's the whole problem, yes.

Director: Why is it a problem?

Builder: Because the young ones will never break free! Who walks away from praise that tells you you're wise?

Director: You?

Builder: I was once wise beyond my years. But I quickly learned I wasn't.

Director: So what did you do?

Builder: I starved myself of praise.

Director: For how long?

Builder: Up until today.

Director: Years and years of accepting no praise?

Builder: Oh, I got praise enough—in spreadsheets and annual reports. But praise directly from people? Not if I could help it.

Senator: That sounds so harsh. Praise is sweet.

Builder: I lost my sweet tooth long ago.

Senator: I don't understand why.

Builder: Praise is an attempt to manipulate. It's an old technique. You tell someone they are what you want them to be.

Senator: So if I tell you you're very considerate of others....

Builder: You hope I'll live up to the praise.

Director: And this works?

Builder: With some? It does. But not with me.

— Flattery

Director: Is there such a thing as honest praise? Praise without other motives?

Builder: Genuine appreciation? Yes, that happens. But not so often for tyrants.

Director: So what do tyrants mostly get? Flattery?

Builder: I hate flattery.

Director: Are you often flattered?

Builder: All the time.

Director: So you walk around feeling great hate?

Builder: I suppose I do.

Director: Do you like feeling great hate?

Builder: It's funny you should ask. It motivates me.

Director: So you do like feeling great hate.

Builder: I do. But it might be best to describe it as terrible contempt.

Director: Why is a flatterer worthy of contempt?

Builder: Because they're excessively insincere.

Director: But if they were moderately insincere?

Builder: I'd like that better.

Director: And would you like it better still if they were sincere?

Builder: Only if moderately so.

Senator: Why only moderately?

Builder: I can't stomach the perfectly sincere.

Director: But still, there's something good about sincerity?

Builder: Yes, of course. It lets me know where someone stands.

Director: That makes it easier to manipulate them?

Builder: Yes.

Director: Is this so even if they blame you rather than praise?

Builder: It certainly is.

Director: Who are you more likely to keep around? Someone who gives you some praise, or someone who gives you some blame?

Builder: The one who gives me blame.

Director: Because it's hard for them to speak what they think?

Builder: Because I want to keep an eye on them.

Director: If you had to surround yourself with one type or the other, which would it be?

Builder: Neither. I'd surround myself with those who have no opinion about me, one way or the other.

Director: You just want people who keep their heads down and do their jobs.

Builder: Precisely.

Senator: You don't like anyone telling you how you're doing?

Builder: Why should I, Senator? I see my results very clearly.

Senator: But don't you ever take advice?

Builder: I took Director's advice, didn't I? And do you know why?

Senator: Why?

Builder: I could tell he had no opinion.

Senator: That or he kept it very well hidden.

Builder: Which amounts to much the same thing.

— The Hidden

Senator: But does it? Don't you want to get at the hidden truth? Don't tyrants long to know just that? I think it drives you crazy when you don't know what people think.

Builder: And why do you think that?

Senator: Because you suspect the worst.

Builder: That no one likes me? That's the least of my worries. But what about you, Senator? You want to be loved. Otherwise why seek those votes? Does it drive you crazy not to know what people think?

Senator: I always want to know what people think. So I encourage sincerity.

Builder: And what does all that sincerity get you?

Senator: Knowledge of what I need to do.

Builder: Yes, because you do what you're told. But I suppose there's an advantage to knowing how many think well or poorly of you.

Senator: What advantage?

Builder: It helps someone like you determine your strength.

Senator: That's all you think people care about, isn't it? How much strength or power they have.

Builder: Mostly? Yes. Though they're not always honest with themselves. Why, you don't care about that?

Senator: I care about knowing myself.

Builder: But isn't the amount of power you have... yourself?

Senator: Director, do you hear this?

Director: I do. But I can't say I'm surprised. I've suspected this about Builder for quite some time.

Builder: Why, what do you think is worth knowing?

Director: About yourself? Everything you can. About others? Well, I certainly think it's important to know how much power a person has. But I'm interested in a person's heart of hearts.

Builder: What they hold most dear?

Director: Yes.

Builder: So that once you know, you can manipulate them accordingly?

Director: That's not what I was thinking.

Builder: Then what?

Director: I want to help them get what they want.

Builder: You'd give everyone what they want? You'd bring their deepest desires up and into the light?

Director: What would be wrong with that?

Builder: People don't always want good things!

Director: Do you want good things?

Builder: Do I? Well....

Director: Is your empire what most would call good?

Builder: They're more likely to call it evil.

Director: But you think it's good.

Builder: Yes, I think it's good.

Director: Tell me something that would be bad.

Senator: I'll tell you, Director. A burning desire for revenge.

Director: Is there any desire in your heart of hearts for revenge, Senator?

Senator: No. But Builder on the other hand....

Director: Builder?

Builder: I'll be honest. I burn for revenge.

Director: Revenge against whom?

Builder: Pretty much everyone.

Director: Except for those who keep their heads down and work?

Builder: Yes, except for them.

— Revenge

Senator: So, Director, do you want to help Builder get what he wants?

Director: His revenge? Sure, why not?

Builder: And how will you do that?

Director: First we have to say why revenge, then what that revenge would be.

Builder: Why revenge? I'm not afraid to tell you two. The world never gave me a chance.

Senator: It never appreciated you for what you are?

Builder: No, I'm not talking about that. It made me claw my way to everything I've got.

Director: How does that make you different than anyone else?

Builder: How? Don't you see how many have it easy? And don't you see how they look down on people like me?

Director: Look down on you for having to try?

Builder: Yes.

Director: I don't know, Builder. Many people admire those who try.

Builder: Not those who've had it handed to them.

Director: Sometimes especially them.

Builder: I don't know about that. But do you know what's worst?

Director: No, tell us.

Builder: They question my motives.

Director: They don't always assume they're good?

Builder: Ha! Not at all. But I'll tell you what this taught me. Motives don't count. Only results. And I have better results than anyone.

Director: And that's your revenge.

Builder: That's my revenge.

Director: Senator, it seems Builder doesn't need our help.

Senator: But he does. He doesn't have the right revenge.

Director: What would be the right revenge?

Senator: Proving his motives are true.

Director: Are they true?

Senator: Maybe once they were.

Builder: My youthful motives? Should I prove they were once true in my heart? But what does it matter? My heart has changed.

Senator: It's blackened, yes. But we can scrape away the char.

Builder: Don't tell me this has to do with love.

Senator: What else can work the wonder?

Builder: Are you suggesting love should be the tool of revenge? What? You don't like it that way?

Director: Maybe it's better to reverse what we're saying. Maybe properly executed revenge, along Senator's lines, is the tool of love.

Builder: So what do I have to do?

Director: See if you can find the old words deep in your heart.

Builder: The words I once spoke to myself? My old motives?

Director: Yes. See if you can resuscitate them.

Builder: Resuscitate words? Ha, ha.

Director: Oh, but please don't laugh. Bringing nearly dead words back to full life is...

Builder: Is what?

Director: ...all but divine.

— Oaths

Builder: How do we bring a word back to life?

Senator: We have to live up to it.

Builder: How do we do that?

Senator: Isn't it obvious?

Builder: Not to me, it isn't.

Director: Maybe this will help. Senator, you took an oath of office, didn't you?

Senator: Yes, of course.

Director: Do you know how to live up to that oath?

Senator: I do.

Director: Can you imagine other oaths, oaths you make to yourself and only yourself?

Senator: I don't have to imagine oaths like that.

Director: What happens if you don't live up to oaths like these?

Senator: You die a little inside.

Director: Now tell us. What if you took an inner oath in ignorance of what it truly means?

Senator: Well, that's a problem.

Director: If you come to learn what it means, can you modify the oath to fit what you know?

Senator: I think you have to.

Builder: Why not just replace it with a new oath?

Senator: It's easier on the psyche to modify rather than replace.

Builder: Why have an oath at all?

Senator: It can help guide us through life.

Builder: Can an oath be a single word?

Senator: Of course.

Builder: Then tell me, Director. What's a good word to steer by?

Director: Everyone will have their own.

Builder: What word do you steer by?

Director: I steer by many words.

Builder: Yes, yes. But what's the main word for you?

Director: Philosophy.

Builder: Do you know what that word means?

Director: I do.

Builder: Then tell us what it means.

Director: And give away my heart? Oh, no, Builder. I'm not in the habit of revealing the secrets of my soul.

Builder: As if philosophy is some great secret.

Director: Alright. I'll open up a bit. Philosophy is the love of wisdom. So you see? There's love in my core.

Builder: Oh, you're just repeating what I said.

Director: And I will again and again. But what do you really think philosophy is?

Builder: A way of having fun with others.

Director: And if that's what it is, do you see anything wrong?

Builder: If it's making fun of others, yes. But if it's having fun together? That seems fine.

Director: Senator, I want you to note. Builder the Terrible is concerned with others' feelings.

Senator: Duly noted. And terribly odd.

— Concern

Director: Yes, odd indeed. Maybe Builder is bringing a word back to life.

Builder: What word?

Director: Concern.

Builder: I've always been concerned.

Director: For those who keep their heads down and work?

Builder: Yes. And, in fact, you might say that's who my empire is for.

Director: Senator, we're hearing something remarkable.

Senator: We certainly are.

Director: Builder is an altruist.

Senator: I never would have guessed.

Director: No, nor I. This is an amazing confession. Tell us, Builder. You said before you love your slaves. Are you saying something different here?

Builder: I am. I love and serve those who keep their heads down and work.

Director: You really serve certain subordinates?

Builder: Ask them and see.

Director: But only subordinates?

Builder: You want me to serve my equals? You and Senator, you mean?

Director: I do. And I want you to let us serve you, too.

Builder: Yes, but I suspect you're a joker in this.

Director: A card that can be whatever card it likes? No, Builder, I wouldn't say that's me. I'm very much what I am, and nothing else.

Builder: And you don't think I'm what I am?

Director: But what are you? And I don't mean to hurt your feelings. Are you a tyrant? Are you a lover of certain employees? Are you misunderstood? What?

Builder: Senator, Director is full of it, isn't he?

Senator: Full of truth? Yes, I'd say he is.

Builder: Oh, you know that's not what I mean.

Senator: Yes, but it's what I mean.

Builder: Director, tell me, and be honest now. Do you think you're full of truth?

Director: I'll tell you what I am at my worst.

Builder: Good! That's what I was hoping to hear.

Director: I'm an echo chamber of truth.

Builder: What does that mean?

Director: When people speak truth in my ear, it echoes around in this head of mine until someone asks me what I think. And, invariably it seems, one of the echoes escapes.

Builder: I don't think that's how it is at all.

Director: How is it?

Builder: You pretend you don't know what you're talking about—until it's time.

Director: And what good does that do?

Builder: You catch your opponent off guard.

Director: Making them more vulnerable?

Builder: Yes.

Director: I'll have to try that some day. But why do you speak of an opponent?

Builder: You know why. You're trying to win.

Director: By sharing the truth? The first to share a new truth wins? Or is it the one who shares the most truth wins? Either way, while I like to win—I'd rather lose. And learn all the more that way.

— Sharing

Senator: Yes, but you won't learn much from tyrants. They don't like to share.

Builder: Because tyrants find no one worth sharing with. Do philosophers?

Director: Philosophers share with one and all.

Builder: I don't believe that for a minute. What do they share?

Director: Their love for wisdom.

Builder: Then share some wisdom with me.

Director: But I didn't say philosophers share wisdom with one and all. I said they share their love for wisdom.

Builder: How do you share a love?

Director: You search together for the object of this love.

Builder: So you'd search for wisdom with me.

Director: And Senator, too.

Builder: Have you searched with others for wisdom before?

Director: I have.

Builder: And what did you find?

Director: I'm still trying to make sense of it all.

Builder: But you can tell if someone is wise?

Director: I can. You, for instance, have a certain sort of wisdom.

Builder: What sort of wisdom?

Senator: I know. It has to do with love. Love for your unambitious, hardworking subordinates.

Builder: So, Director, you love my love?

Senator: He loves it so long as you share the good things of your rule with those you love.

Builder: And I do. They benefit when I do well. I see to that.

Director: And so their loyalty grows?

Builder: Yes, it does.

Director: Then that seems wise. Senator, you have subordinates, don't you? People who keep their heads down and work?

Senator: I do.

Director: Do they benefit when you do well?

Senator: Of course they do. Though I can't give them more money like Builder.

Director: So how do they benefit?

Senator: Through satisfaction.

Director: Ah. Is satisfaction more important than money?

Senator: In my world it is.

Director: And in your world, Builder?

Builder: Money satisfies. What can I say?

Director: Does Builder share more than you do, Senator? He's saying he gives what you give and more.

Senator: I doubt his people's satisfaction is as great as my people's satisfaction. But I'd like to know this, Builder. If you had to choose, money with no satisfaction or satisfaction alone—which would you prefer?

Builder: Oh, that's an unrealistic choice. But okay, I'll admit. I'd prefer satisfaction.

Senator: Now we're speaking truth.

Builder: We are. And the thing that satisfies me, satisfies all.

Director: And what satisfies you?

Builder: But you already know. The exercise of power.

Senator: But what about the satisfaction of the ones you employ, the ones who keep their heads down and work?

Builder: I delegate small amounts of power to them.

Senator: And that's enough?

Builder: For most? Sure. But for those who long for more? I promote or fire, depending.

— Depending

Senator: Depending on what?

Builder: On whether they know what to do with this power.

Senator: And what should they do with it?

Builder: Use it to good effect.

Senator: Help grow your empire, you mean.

Builder: What else? And if they do, they get more, and more.

Director: Until they reach their full potential?

Builder: Exactly so.

Director: So what do you think, Senator? Wouldn't you like to work for a company like this? One that rewards performance with power?

Senator: Yes, Director. But toward what end?

Builder: What do you mean?

Senator: Is it power for the sake of power?

Builder: Why not?

Senator: Because that's... amoral!

Builder: Power has to be for the sake of something else?

Senator: Yes, like making people's lives better.

Builder: Those I promote have better lives. Ask them and see.

Senator: I'm not sure they're the sort of people I'd like to meet.

Builder: And that makes you a snob.

Senator: A snob? How so?

Builder: Snobs look down on those who do what they would do, too, if circumstances were changed.

Senator: So what we do depends on our circumstances?

Builder: Not wholly. I know people with circumstances like mine who ended up with nothing.

Director: What makes the difference?

Builder: Ambition to succeed.

Director: What's the key to ambition?

Builder: There is no key. Ambition can't be reduced to something else. You have it or you don't.

Senator: Oh, I don't believe that one bit.

Builder: So what do you think is the key?

Senator: Longing for immortality, the immortality of fame.

— Fame

Director: What is fame?

Senator: A desire to be known.

Director: I want you to know me. Is that the desire we mean?

Builder: You know that's not fame.

Director: What is fame? To have lots of people know me?

Builder: To have everyone know you.

Director: And you've come pretty close to that. You must be proud.

Builder: Oh, stop with the nonsense. Tell us what you think about fame.

Director: You can be famous for many reasons. Having power is one.

Builder: What's another?

Director: Being famous for having fame.

Builder: Ha, ha.

Director: Yes, it's laughable. But tell us this. Do those with fame necessarily have power?

Builder: No, not necessarily.

Director: But can't fame be turned into power?

Builder: That takes a certain skill.

Director: I wonder what that skill is. But let's save that for another time. How else should we describe fame?

Builder: What do you mean?

Director: Is it enough for everyone to know your name?

Builder: They have to know what that name means.

Director: Is it in your power to make them know?

Builder: In my case? Yes.

Director: What does your name mean? Fear?

Builder: You're being ridiculous again.

Director: Am I? Senator, what do you think?

Senator: I sometimes wonder what my name means.

Builder: If you have to wonder, it can't mean much.

Senator: That's not true at all. My name might mean fairness and respect for the law.

Builder: But why would you have to wonder about that? Don't you know if you're fair and full of respect?

Senator: Respect, yes. But I might think I'm fair—and someone might prove me wrong.

Director: What would you do then?

Senator: Change my ways.

Builder: If you were powerful, you wouldn't have to change your ways.

Director: No one can prove the powerful wrong?

Builder: No, it's not that. It's that no one can make you change.

Senator: But I'd want to change. I want my name to mean fairness.

Builder: Fair, unfair—it all depends who you ask.

Director: Builder, what does your name mean?

Builder: When people hear my name I want it to mean respect.

Senator: Your respect for them?

Builder: No, their respect for me.

Director: Respect for your power. Fear of your power.

Builder: Oh, why are you hung up on fear?

Director: Because mere mortals like me fear when confronted with a fact like you. Or are you saying there's nothing in you to fear?

Builder: There's nothing for you to fear.

Director: And yet I still fear.

Builder: Why?

Director: Because I fear for you.

— Fear 2

Builder: Why would you ever fear for me?

Director: What if I told you I worry that fame might swallow you up?

Builder: And what if I tell you I can't think of a better way to go?

Director: To die?

Builder: Yes, to die.

Director: I'd rather die with my friends.

Senator: Director has a good point. Dying with friends is best.

Builder: Like in a desperate last stand?

Senator: Yes. I'd like to go that way.

Director: And you, Builder? With all of your fame, if you could choose, would you like to die in bed?

Builder: No, I'd like to die while fighting.

Director: Fighting for more fame?

Builder: And fighting for revenge.

Director: But why bother with fame? Fame does you no good when you're dead, you know.

Builder: Then I'll be sure to be as famous as can be, while I'm still alive.

Director: And what good comes of that?

Builder: Of fame? Ha, ha.

Director: No, really. What good comes of fame?

Builder: For those who know? Power comes of fame.

Director: Yes, we were just talking about this. We said it takes a certain skill to translate one into the other. What is that skill?

Builder: I don't think there's a name for it.

Director: Maybe political scientists know what it is.

Senator: They talk about name recognition, and how it translates into votes.

Director: Really? Just because someone knows your name they'll grant you power?

Builder: You'd be surprised what people will grant.

Director: I accept that people vote for names they know. Who would vote for a name they don't know? But what if we're not talking about votes? What good is fame?

Builder: People listen to you when you're famous.

Director: Yes, that occurred to me. But then I remembered you never speak to the people. So if you're getting power from your fame, it's not from that.

Builder: I'm not talking about people at large. Specific people listen.

Director: Why?

Builder: Because they're awed by fame.

Director: Ah, fear once again. Now I think I understand. Fame is a tool for fear.

Senator: Yes, but not everyone wants to be feared.

Director: Is there anything that everyone wants?

Senator: From fame? I think people just think it's good.

Builder: But everyone knows power is good.

Director: You'd take power over fame?

Builder: Of course I would. Do you know my favorite god? Poseidon.

Senator: Why is that your favorite god?

Builder: Because he lives deep down at the bottom of the sea. Seen by none, he shakes the Earth.

Director: And you want to shake the Earth.

Builder: The point is I'd rather shake than be seen, if I had to choose.

Director: Shake the Earth in revenge.

Builder: Yes.

Director: But wouldn't it be better to be seen, as well? Wouldn't that make your victory complete?

Builder: You're a sort of tempter, aren't you?

Director: Tempter? What am I tempting you toward?

Builder: To come up from the bottom of the sea. But why should I? Poseidon is famous enough even though he's rarely seen. And so am I.

Director: Yes, but I'm not so much trying to tempt you as I'm trying to find out what's really in your heart of hearts.

Builder: I told you I want revenge.

Director: Yes, but I think you want more.

Builder: Fame.

Director: No, not fame.

Builder: You're going to tell me what's in my heart of hearts?

Director: I'm looking for something that rings true.

Builder: Power. Power is truly what I want.

Director: Hmm. No.

Builder: No? What, then?

Director: Love. You want love. But you're afraid.

— Love 3

Builder: Why do we keep coming back to love?

Director: We're zeroing in on what's in your heart.

Builder: Then tell me. Why am I afraid of love?

Director: Why is anyone afraid of love? You don't want to get hurt.

Builder: And all my power is nothing more than a wall to protect me?

Director: Is it?

Builder: No, of course not. And you, is philosophy really in your heart of hearts?

Director: It really is.

Builder: Why do I sense you're lying?

Director: Because that's what you want to believe.

Builder: And why would I want to believe that?

Director: Because you want our hearts to be the same.

Builder: Why?

Director: I don't know. Because you think close friends should be like?

Builder: You don't think of me as a close friend.

Senator: Why can't we give the simple answer?

Builder: And what's the simple answer?

Senator: You want your hearts to be the same—because misery loves company.

Director: Are you in misery, Builder?

Builder: No one loves as a tyrant loves.

Director: How does a tyrant love?

Builder: With the utmost loyalty.

Director: And there's passion in the loyalty?

Builder: Of course.

Director: And maybe... a touch of madness, too?

Builder: And maybe that, too.

Senator: Wait. What are you two talking about? Madness in loyalty?

Builder: Oh, Senator. Don't you know? You can be mad in how loyal you are.

Senator: I don't understand.

Builder: I'm not surprised. So let me explain. You can be loyal to the point of self·destruction. That's the madness Director sees.

Senator: But why would you want to be mad?

Builder: It's a badge of honor. You wouldn't understand.

Senator: But your loyalty lies only with yourself.

Builder: If that's all you can see, then I can't help you here.

Senator: Tell us where it lies.

Director: It has to do with his revenge.

Builder: Yes. But how did you know?

Director: I guessed. Your revenge is for you, and it's not for you.

Builder: My revenge is for someone else. A friend I loved dearly.

Senator: You love this friend no more?

Builder: My friend is dead.

Senator: I'm sorry. What happened to... him?

Builder: Yes, him. He was killed in a terrible accident.

Director: Can you tell us more?

Builder: The world, Director. The world conspired to keep us apart. And it drove him too far. That's all I'll say.

— The World

Director: Why did the world conspire to keep you apart?

Builder: Because the world can't stand anything too good.

Director: Out of envy?

Builder: Yes.

Director: So you take your revenge on the world.

Builder: Every single day.

Director: But surely there are those who aren't jealous when it comes to these things.

Builder: There are. I recognize them right away. That's what I see in you and Senator, here.

Director: So you'd take no revenge on us.

Builder: None.

Director: But the rest, you strike them with all the power you've got?

Builder: I do.

Director: And your lust for power comes from this desire for revenge?

Builder: Yes.

Director: Do you think it's that way with others?

Builder: What do you mean?

Director: You're not alone in lusting for power. But do the others lust for revenge?

Builder: I don't know. I've never thought about it before.

Senator: People can simply think power is good, no revenge involved.

Builder: People, sure. But if you lust for power, crave it—revenge or not—you do more than think it's good. There's something darker here.

Director: Do you want it dark?

Builder: I do.

Senator: Why?

Builder: Because I know others would object if they knew the extent of my desire.

Senator: And with good reason.

Builder: What makes a reason good?

Senator: It's for the benefit of all.

Builder: All the world, sure. But people who lust for power don't care about that.

Senator: And so they hide in the dark.

Director: Do you think they'd do well to expose themselves to the light?

Senator: I do. And that's how their craving becomes simple ambition.

Builder: Simple ambition? There's no such thing. Besides, I hide only as much as philosophy does.

Director: What's this?

Builder: I maneuver people into traps, just like you.

Senator: But your traps are about revenge. That's nothing like what Director does.

Builder: Still, trapping is trapping. And that's how what I do and what Director does relate.

Senator: But are you suggesting something more? Are you suggesting philosophy, too, is somehow bent on revenge?

Builder: Is it, Director?

Director: Philosophers are as human as the rest of us. Have certain philosophers plotted revenge? Probably.

Senator: Yes, but do they maneuver people the way Builder does?

Director: Again, philosophers are human. But Builder seeks one thing while philosophers largely seek another.

Builder: What do I seek?

Director: To maneuver people to their doom.

Builder: And you?

Director: To help them find a better way.

— Happiness 3

Builder: Yes, but what's a better way?

Senator: I'll answer that. It has to do with happiness.

Builder: Happiness is the dream of fools.

Senator: I thought you were happy because you love what you do.

Builder: There's happiness, and then there's happiness.

Director: So you're not truly happy? That makes me wonder.

Builder: About what?

Director: Whether longing for power and happiness are mutually exclusive.

Builder: That's a good question. I think they are.

Director: Is that because when you long for power, there's never really enough? Never a point where you stop?

Builder: And this interferes with happiness, yes.

Director: Because when you're happy, you're happy—and that's enough.

Builder: Right. And that will never be my way. Unless you maneuver me into a different aim.

Director: You can't be tricked into wanting something else.

Builder: But you believe I can be persuaded?

Director: It's happened before.

Builder: So how does the persuasion work?

Director: The unhappy see the way to happiness.

Builder: And you believe you've seen the way for me?

Director: It doesn't work like that.

Builder: Then how does it work?

Director: Philosophers help friends show themselves the way.

Builder: So you're going to help me show myself the way to happiness.

Director: If that's what you want, I can try.

Builder: And what about my revenge?

Director: That will never make you happy.

Builder: Then happiness isn't what I want.

Senator: At bottom, we all want happiness, Builder.

Builder: That shows how little you know the heart.

— Arrogance

Senator: You'd really rather have power and revenge than happiness?

Builder: I really would. Unless Director helps me see a better way.

Senator: I can show you that way. It's so obvious I can't believe you haven't thought of it yourself.

Builder: Well, this ought to be good. Show me, Senator.

Senator: Happiness is the best revenge.

Builder: I can see how you might think that. But you're not quite right. Ruining someone's happiness is the best revenge.

Senator: So you'd like to ruin the happiness of the world?

Builder: With certain exceptions, yes.

Director: But what about your buildings?

Builder: What about them?

Director: Are they the tools of revenge?

Builder: In more ways than one. Do you know how?

Director: Tell us.

Builder: Do you agree my buildings are magnificent?

Director: I do.

Builder: Well, in all their magnificence—they're monuments to arrogance.

Senator: Your arrogance?

Builder: No, the arrogance of the investors and occupants.

Director: Your buildings support and enhance their arrogance.

Builder: And where do you think that eventually leads?

Director: With a little encouragement from you? To a fall.

Builder: Precisely.

Senator: Oh, I don't believe for a minute you make all these people fall. But even if you did, that's hardly ruining the happiness of the world. You're more innocent than you let on.

Builder: I wreck the whole world—their world, whenever I can. There's nothing innocent in that.

Senator: True. But you seem to me to be robbing from the rich and giving to the poor, or at least acting in that spirit.

Builder: No, I couldn't care less about that. The poor can take care of themselves. More so when the arrogant rich are out of the way.

Senator: But then you do see yourself as helping the poor.

Builder: Maybe certain members of the poor, sure. But in that sense I also help certain members of the rich.

Director: Those who are willing to keep their heads down and work.

Builder: Those people, exactly.

Director: But what if they work but lift up their heads?

Builder: It's not good to see too much.

Director: As you have? Do you wish you could unsee what you saw?

Builder: That's a rather personal question, don't you think?

Director: Even if it is, I thought we were dealing as friends.

Builder: And friends share personal things?

Director: Haven't you done so already? Or would you undo what you've done?

Builder: It's time for you to share.

Director: I've shared personal things tonight.

Builder: What personal things?

Director: Philosophy and its meaning to me.

Builder: That's not personal. You have to share something more.

Director: The thing most precious to me isn't personal enough for you?

Builder: What's so precious about asking annoying questions? I do that all the time.

Director: I think there's a difference between our questions.

Builder: Oh? Do tell.

Director: When I ask, I hope the answer will surprise.

Builder: And when I ask?

Director: You want to annoy.

— Difference

Builder: What does this difference mean?

Director: I think it's the difference between being happy or not.

Builder: Now you have to say more.

Director: I will. When I'm surprised, I'm pleased. It's an opportunity to learn. But you don't like surprises.

Builder: Why do you think that is?

Director: You think you've got it all figured out.

Builder: But so do you.

Director: However that may be, I'm open to being wrong.

Builder: And you think I'm certain I'm right? And you're right! But what could you be wrong about?

Director: What certain human beings think.

Builder: Why do you care what they think?

Director: That's what philosophers do.

Builder: They care? Ha, ha.

Senator: What's wrong with caring?

Builder: I'll share a secret with you. You'll go insane if you try to know what people think.

Senator: Then how do you deal with them?

Builder: You focus on what they do. Director knows this. I think his philosophical concern for thought is just a pose.

Senator: Then why does he do what he does?

Builder: He likes to talk. It makes him happy. So that's what he does.

Senator: What do you like to do?

Builder: I like to punish the bad.

Director: The seeming bad or the bad?

Builder: The bad, often known as the good.

Director: How do you keep the two straight?

Builder: I have to get close and study their actions.

Director: And if they do good things?

Builder: I reward them for their effort.

Senator: And if they do bad?

Builder: I get to do what I like.

— A Jury

Director: But I wonder. If they appear bad from a distance, but when studied up close prove to be good, don't you want to help them change how they seem from afar?

Builder: Why should they change how they seem?

Senator: So the court of public opinion doesn't wrongfully convict them.

Builder: The great jury of their peers? What do they know?

Senator: They're supposed to know truth beyond a reasonable doubt.

Builder: Ha! Public opinion often comes down to a whim.

Director: And what about with you?

Builder: What do you mean?

Director: When you decide to punish, do you hold a sort of trial?

Builder: I do. And I'm judge, jury, and executioner three.

Director: And you only execute when guilt is beyond a reasonable doubt?

Builder: Yes.

Senator: But how do you know what's reasonable?

Builder: Senator, I see you'll be a philosopher yet.

Director: Yes, but how do you know?

Builder: I'm a reasonable man. If I have no reasonable doubt, I know.

Senator: But how do you know you're a reasonable man? Maybe lust for power and revenge has made you mad, unreasonable.

Builder: Then you tell me what it means to be reasonable.

Senator: It means to form your judgments by a logical process.

Director: That's funny, Senator. I don't know if that's what most people would say.

Senator: What would they say?

Director: Being reasonable is to be moderate or fair.

Senator: Well, Builder certainly isn't moderate when it comes to power or revenge. So the question is whether he's fair.

Builder: By fair do you mean beautiful, or just?

Director: Can the immoderate be beautiful?

Senator: No, and I don't see how they can be just.

Director: So poor Builder isn't fair.

Senator: Which means he's in no position to judge.

Builder: But I form my judgments by a logical process!

Senator: Describe your process.

Builder: If someone contributes to a world that tears good friends apart, that someone should pay.

Director: That's logic enough for me.

Senator: What? That's hardly any logic at all!

Director: You want it all spelled out?

Senator: Yes. That's what a judge does when giving instructions to a jury. He or she spells it all out.

Director: So you, Builder, being both judge and jury, must make yourself clear on these things.

Builder: But I am clear on these things.

Director: Then tell us what it means to contribute to a bad world, and so on and so on.

Builder: To support certain ideas. To act on those ideas.

Director: Senator, do we need to dive deeper and ask what these certain ideas are?

Senator: Of course we do.

Builder: The simplest way I can describe them is to say they rank friendship incorrectly.

Director: How should friendship be ranked?

Builder: As the highest thing in the world.

Director: Is that good enough for you, Senator?

Senator: Yes, that's good enough for me.

Director: Now, do we need to define tearing friends apart?

Senator: No, I understand that well enough.

Director: Then what's left is what it means to pay.

Senator: It means to be the object of revenge.

Director: Then the instructions to the jury are complete. We await the verdict on Builder.

Builder: What am I on trial for?

Director: For choosing power over friends.

— Friends

Builder: No. Friendship is what matters to me.

Senator: But all you have is revenge for your friend.

Builder: You two are my friends.

Director: Would you choose power over us?

Builder: It doesn't come down to that. Our friendship doesn't interfere with my power.

Senator: If it did, we wouldn't be friends?

Builder: Yes, that might be true. But so what? What if, what if—keep asking that and you'll drive yourself mad.

Senator: But you're still saying power is more important than friends. And you're acting on this.

Builder: No, Senator, you don't understand. Tell me. What makes a friend?

Senator: Love.

Builder: Yes, love. But what else?

Senator: You tell me.

Builder: Shared interests. Power is in my interest. And my friends can share that interest with me.

Senator: And if they don't?

Builder: We can't be friends.

Director: Just to be clear, you're saying love without interest isn't enough?

Builder: I'm saying something more profound. I'm saying love without interest isn't love.

Senator: What is it?

Builder: Puppy love, at best.

Senator: Oh, that's ridiculous. I know plenty of people who love against their interest.

Director: The love isn't in their interest?

Senator: No, other things that come with the love aren't in their interest.

Builder: Then the love won't last. How many friendships go against the friends' interests? Tell me that.

Director: Builder has a point.

Senator: Then let me ask you, Director. I'd say you and I have become friends tonight. What's your interest in me?

Director: Your wisdom.

Builder: You see? He knows his interest. So be honest with us now, Senator. What's your interest in Director?

Senator: I have no interest in him. We're simply friends.

Builder: Well, you can't argue with stupidity. Director, what's your interest in me?

Director: What brought me here tonight? Your power.

Builder: Why did my power bring you here?

Director: Because power fascinates philosophers.

Builder: Why?

Director: Why does it fascinate anyone?

Builder: Yes, but you're not anyone. Why does it fascinate you?

Director: Because of its potential.

Builder: What potential?

Director: For good and bad.

Builder: And you value a friendship with me because you hope to influence me here?

Director: No, I value a friendship with you because you fascinate me.

Builder: You wouldn't try to persuade me toward the good?

Director: Of course I would. You can persuade those who fascinate you.

Builder: But how do you know what's good? Because it's good for you?

Director: I like to think what's good for me is good for others, too.

Builder: How do you know if it is?

Director: I have to look into their hearts.

Builder: And what do you hope to see?

Director: The reasons for and against.

— Arguments

Builder: Do people really have reasons in their hearts?

Director: All people? I don't know. But many do.

Builder: That's a problem.

Director: How so?

Builder: The reasons should be in their heads.

Director: What's the difference between a reason in the heart and one in the head?

Builder: The one in the heart is hard to dislodge if it proves bad.

Senator: I think he has a point.

Director: He does. But tell us, Builder. Does it make a difference if someone acts from the heart or the head?

Builder: An act is an act. What matters is the effect.

Senator: And some effects are good and some are bad?

Builder: Yes, of course. But not in the sense you mean.

Senator: What sense do I mean?

Builder: Knowing you? You're talking about the moral good and bad.

Senator: And what are you talking about?

Builder: Whether it's the effect I want.

Director: In other words, whether it's good for you.

Builder: Yes.

Director: Do you ever question that good?

Builder: You don't win an empire like mine through self-doubt.

Director: That must be the reason I don't have an empire.

Builder: You question yourself?

Director: All the time.

Builder: Even concerning philosophy?

Director: Even so. I question how effective my philosophy is.

Builder: Your philosophy? You don't have a philosophy.

Director: So you see my trouble.

Builder: You need to have a teaching if you hope to gain power over the minds of women and men.

Director: But that's not my hope.

Builder: What is your hope?

Senator: I know. It's to liberate the minds of women and men.

Director: No, not that either.

Builder: Then what?

Director: To exercise minds and make them strong. But I have trouble even here.

Builder: Why?

Director: Those who train with me start with the exercises I favor.

Builder: Why do you favor them?

Director: Because they're good for me. But they're not always good for all others.

Builder: They need to find exercises of their own.

Director: Yes. And here's the problem. Some of them don't.

Builder: Why wouldn't they?

Director: Because they find my exercises easy, though they're difficult for me.

Builder: And so they think they're very strong, stronger than their coach. These are interesting things, Director. I have similar experiences.

Director: Oh?

Builder: I often come across people who believe they're powerful when they're not. But I don't doubt I can help them. I always set them straight.

Director: Through reasoned argument?

Builder: No. And I think that's your problem. You rely too much on reason. Reason is fine, but you need something more. That's what naked power is for. I set my very real power against their imagined power, and win every time.

Director: The loss teaches them the truth?

Builder: Yes, and there's no finer teacher, in the end.

— Teachers

Senator: Yes, but neither of you is talking about having a teaching.

Builder: What do you want us to teach?

Senator: You could work with Director to create a philosophy of power.

Builder: That's already been done.

Senator: Then how about a philosophy of friendship?

Builder: Senator, what's the point? I know you can't really want a teaching from me. You want one from Director. But he doesn't want to give you one on his own. So you hope he'll agree to work with me to conjure one up.

Director: I'm sorry, Senator. But I'm just not the teaching sort.

Senator: Who is the teaching sort?

Director: Someone who believes that he or she has knowledge worth sharing.

Builder: I believe I have knowledge worth sharing. But I don't want to share.

Senator: And you, Director, you don't believe you have worthwhile knowledge?

Director: Well, maybe in a sense.

Builder: What sense? You either have it or you don't.

Director: I have exercises I might share, a process if you will. But, still, I'm leery.

Senator: Why be leery if the process is good? A process is a kind of knowledge, you know.

Director: Yes, but as I've said, the process might not be as good for others as it is for me.

Senator: That's a chance you have to take.

Director: Thanks for encouraging me. But now I have to ask. Why don't you teach?

Senator: I would if I had more time. Maybe when I retire.

Builder: What would you teach?

Senator: Government or political science.

Builder: Stick with government. Political science is all about power.

Senator: And government isn't?

Builder: In a government course you can teach all the rules and ways. But in a political science course, in a course on the science of politics, you'd be less than scientific if you don't tell it like it is—and it's all about power.

Senator: Then you should teach the course with me, since power is what you know.

Builder: Teach innocents the way of the world? Why would I do that?

Senator: If the world works as you think, the more that know it the better.

Builder: Why?

Senator: Because there are things we need to get done, and knowing how to do them is key.

Builder: But what if I don't want the things you want done? Look. The best way to teach power is to give some to the student. That's what I do. But I only give power to those who'll do what I want, who'll further my end.

Senator: And what about their ends?

Builder: They're in harmony with mine or the students have to break away. And I admire them when they do.

Senator: Just as Director admires those who find their own exercises to strengthen their minds.

Builder: Yes, we have this in common. And that's one of the reasons I would give power to him.

Senator: But your ends differ greatly.

Director: What's my end?

Senator: Healthy minds.

Director: And Builder's?

Senator: His empire, and what it allows him to do.

— Doing

Builder: And that's the thing. Doing. Not teaching. Doing.

Senator: Teaching is a type of doing.

Builder: You may as well say sitting is a type of standing. But I worry about our friend Director, here. I worry he's not doing enough.

Director: What would you have me do?

Builder: Work for me.

Director: Doing what?

Builder: More of what you've done. Make my headaches go away.

Director: I have headaches of my own that need attention.

Builder: Nothing makes headaches go away like success.

Director: What is success?

Builder: Ah, the philosopher again. Success is achieving what you want to achieve.

Director: What if what you want is bad?

Builder: Bad, or bad for you?

Director: Does it matter?

Builder: Of course it matters. Pick one.

Director: Bad for you.

Builder: If you want what's bad for you, then you're a fool.

Director: Are you successful if you achieve your end, even though it's bad for you?

Builder: That's a trick question.

Senator: Oh, come on. The answer has to be no. And so we need to modify your definition. Success is achieving something good.

Builder: But good by whose lights?

Director: Whose lights would you prefer?

Builder: Only my own.

Director: What about your investors?

Builder: My investors? Ha! They expect a certain building to be built. And I build that building. But things don't always end up the way they'd like.

Director: What do you mean? The buildings aren't good?

Builder: No, the buildings are great. But on the financial side of things, certain investors don't do so well.

Senator: You make that happen as revenge?

Builder: I do what I can. You'd be surprised what kinds of crazy deals you can arrange.

Director: Especially when greed is involved.

Builder: Especially then.

Director: That's something remarkable about you. I don't think you're driven by greed.

Builder: No, money is a tool, that's all. I want lots of it, yes. But it serves the greater end.

Director: Revenge for your friend.

Builder: Revenge for my friend.

— Living

Senator: And so you live for revenge.

Builder: At least I know what I live for.

Senator: And I don't?

Builder: I think it's not so simple for you.

Senator: Oh? Do tell.

Builder: You're a slave to votes. But no one wants to be a slave. So it's complicated.

Senator: How? In detail.

Builder: With enough votes you believe you'll set yourself free. But that's a lie.

Senator: And what's the truth?

Builder: Your slavery only grows. The more votes you have, the more votes you need. And when you have those votes, you need the votes of your peers. You want legislation to bear your name.

Senator: What's wrong with that?

Builder: Did you notice that none of my buildings carries my name?

Senator: I haven't kept up on all you've built.

Builder: None of them does.

Senator: So what's your point?

Builder: Truth be told? I don't care much about fame.

Senator: And I do?

Builder: Of course you do. That's why you want the laws in your name.

Senator: But what's so bad about that? What reason would you rather a legislator have for passing a law?

Builder: I thought it was all about the public good.

Senator: It is about the public good. But sometimes we need something more to sustain us. Working for the public is hard.

Builder: Working for yourself is hard. But you don't see me whining about fame.

Senator: Do you see me whining? I'm telling you honestly what I want, and why I want it.

Builder: And I've done the same.

Senator: But what I want is good. What you want is bad.

Builder: And the badness sustains me without hope of fame? More people should be bad.

Senator: Director, what are your thoughts here?

Director: Fame, no fame—it doesn't really matter. Living is what counts.

Builder: Yes. That's the point. And when do you live, Senator? When you're on campaign? When you're cajoling your peers?

Senator: I live in it all.

Builder: Well, lucky you.

Director: Don't you live in it all?

Builder: I do. But I live most when I have my revenge.

Senator: Revenge is fleeting.

Builder: So are your laws.

Senator: Laws can live a hundred years or more.

Builder: Certain trees can live a lot longer than that. But you don't see me trying to attach my name to them.

Senator: Look, I too believe living, not fame, is the point. But I want both. I want to live my life in the here and now—and I want my name to live on in the law.

Builder: What a foolish want. Don't you know your laws can be repealed?

Senator: Of course I do.

Builder: Then you're hoping for some luck?

Senator: Well....

Builder: You are hoping for some luck. Or you pretend to yourself that your name living on won't take luck. I don't hope for luck. I train myself for skill. Much like Director, here.

Senator: Yes, but Director and I have something in common. We want to help others.

Builder: You're altruists? Ha, ha. Director?

Director: I wouldn't call myself an altruist.

Builder: You're an egoist.

Director: I'm no '-ist'.

Senator: Then what are you?

Builder: I know what he is. He's a man who stands on his own.

Senator: We all have to stand on our own.

Builder: No, Senator. Very few of us stand on our own. And the rest? They lean on others.

— Standing

Director: Does this leaning affect their political views?

Builder: Does it? Of course it does! You can't be a neutral judge when you lean.

Senator: And you're a judge without bias?

Builder: I judge things for what they are.

Senator: And you, Director?

Builder: Oh, he's neutral, too. But he doesn't admit it.

Director: Why wouldn't I admit it?

Builder: Because you're afraid of seeming amoral like me.

Director: Are you amoral? Maybe. But it seems to me you were once highly moral.

Builder: How so?

Director: Friendship requires moral ground to stand on. Didn't you know?

Senator: I think Director is right. Without morals what kind of friend can you be?

Builder: You're a slippery one, Director.

Director: How is speaking in the name of morality slippery?

Builder: Because you're not being honest.

Director: You think I really don't believe friendship requires moral ground? Then tell us. How can the amoral be friends?

Builder: You and I are friends. That's all the proof you need.

Director: But if you really are amoral, I won't work with you.

Senator: Bravo, Director!

Builder: Now you've gone and stirred up Senator. But I see your game. You're going to lean on him.

Director: And I hope he leans on me. That's what friends are for. Or have you forgotten?

Builder: Don't you dare question my memory of my friend.

Director: I'll question that and more.

Senator: Gentlemen, let's not get too heated.

Builder: Neither of us is getting heated.

Director: No, you're cold with anger.

Senator: Director is simply saying friends should lean on one another. And I agree. Don't you?

Builder: Oh, I agree. But I'll note one thing. If you stand perfectly straight, you can't have any friends.

Director: Why not?

Builder: Because who could stand with you for long?

Director: I think Builder is bent on causing trouble tonight.

Builder: It seems that way because I stand up straight on my own.

Director: And you're sure that's why you're alone?

Builder: Positive.

Director: And if alone, asocial?

Builder: Yes.

Director: And if asocial, amoral?

Builder: You seem to understand quite well.

Director: I'm not sure I do understand. That's why I'm asking questions. But there's something holding me back.

Builder: What?

Director: It's a feeling I have.

Builder: Don't trust feelings, Director. They get you nowhere.

Director: Perhaps. But I can't help feeling that standing on your own is as moral a stance as you can take

Builder: Call it what you will. That doesn't change the facts.

Senator: It's a fact that we all need help from time to time.

Builder: You mean, we all need to lean. Well, I don't. And Director only pretends.

Director: Why would I do that?

Builder: You're trying to confuse things to cover your tracks.

Director: Well, say what you will. But I intend to lean on Senator, here.

Senator: And I will lean on you.

Builder: How touching. And preposterous. But I think I know what this is all about.

Director: Enlighten us.

Builder: You want to turn things on their head. You'd make the amoral seem moral.

Director: And how would I do that? By proclamation?

Senator: Never mind Builder, Director. As you said, he's bent on trouble.

Builder: Am I? Then tell me this. Have you heard of moral support?

Senator: Of course I have.

Builder: What do you think it means? Ha! What's the matter? Can't you say?

Director: Builder, talk like this goes nowhere. So let's start over again. When you stand alone, are you moral or amoral? Which is it?

Builder: It makes no difference what I say.

Director: Then you'll just leave us perplexed?

Builder: Oh, you're not perplexed.

Director: How do you know?

Builder: I can see you, Director.

Director: You can see into my heart and mind? Maybe I should lean on you.

Builder: Yes, maybe you should.

Director: But would you consent to lean on me in turn? What? No answer?

Builder: Who do you think you are?

Director: That's your answer?

Builder: No, it's a question. Who do you think you are?

Director: I like to think I'm a friend.

— Nerve

Builder: He risks my fury and now he's my friend. I'll say it again. The man has nerve.

Director: And you have nerve. More nerve than I.

Builder: Why do you say that?

Director: Not because I want to flatter you. You're more courageous.

Builder: How so?

Director: You stand up to those you hate.

Builder: But you stood up to me.

Director: But I don't hate you.

Builder: What are you trying to imply? That it's harder to stand up to those you hate? I think the opposite is true. It's harder to stand up to those you love.

Director: Why?

Builder: Because you risk losing them.

Senator: So a little courage here and there with them is best.

Director: I'll take that as good advice.

Builder: Don't be ridiculous. More courage is always better than less. Senator believes what he says is true. But you, Director, you're just playing.

Director: And shouldn't friends play?

Senator: Of course they should play.

Builder: What if the play disguises an attack?

Senator: What attack?

Builder: Funny you should ask. This whole night has been one great big attack on me. But no one is attacking you. Why do you think that is?

Senator: I don't know. You deserve it more?

Builder: I'll tell you why. It's because no one really loves you here.

Director: Are you proud of yourself? Are you proud for telling a rotten lie?

Builder: I'm proud for telling the truth. Which is more than I can say for you.

Director: How do you have the nerve to say who I love?

Builder: I have more nerve than you can imagine.

Director: I can imagine quite a bit. And I'll tell you—you fall short.

Builder: Who has more nerve than I?

Director: Someone who stands by a friend, even newly won. Senator, here, is such a one.

Senator: Director, please.

Director: But it's true. Builder forgets. Loyalty, true loyalty, takes courage—and a rare sort at that. If Senator stands by me, his party might lose precious funds. Am I wrong?

Senator: No, you're perfectly right.

Director: Are you willing to lose those funds?

Senator: I am.

Director: No matter what it means for your career, your fame?

Senator: No matter.

Director: And I suspect this, Builder. His career and fame are almost as important to him as your empire is to you. But he's willing to give them up for a friend.

Builder: What haven't I given up for my friend?

Director: What haven't you given up? Maybe not much. But you gave up the most important thing. Friends.

— Friends 2

Builder: Then tell me how I can be your friend.

Director: You must climb the mountain of my soul.

Builder: I should have known. So what's my soul to you? A hill?

Director: Do you really want to know?

Builder: Yes.

Director: Your soul is a plain.

Builder: A plain?

Director: No matter where you look, all around, there's nothing but level revenge.

Builder: My soul is boring?

Director: Well, you are a monomaniac.

Builder: So what do you suggest I do?

Senator: I know what you should do. Trust the power of love.

Builder: And what, love will break up the plain? But love is a drain.

Senator: How so?

Builder: No friend I'll find will have power like me.

Senator: And?

Builder: They'll gain while I lose.

Senator: Lose?

Builder: I'll use my power in service to my friend. But what will they have for me?

Senator: You're missing the point. We always gain by putting our power to good use.

Builder: Yes, but what's good use?

Director: Helping a friend.

Builder: I want to hedge.

Director: Why?

Builder: Because there are friends, and then there are friends.

Director: Just as there's truth, and then there's truth?

Builder: As we've said.

Senator: But truth is certainly truth. And friends are certainly friends.

— Pigs and Horses

Builder: But the fact is we all distinguish between friends and very good friends.

Senator: Of course we do. But both are still friends.

Builder: As distinct from acquaintances and enemies?

Senator: And everyone else, sure.

Builder: But don't you sometimes...

Senator: Sometimes what?

Builder: ...invite your enemies to be friends?

Senator: Why would I do that?

Builder: Haven't you heard the saying? 'Keep your friends close and your enemies closer.'

Senator: Of course I've heard that saying. But I don't believe we should call our enemies friends.

Builder: Why not?

Senator: That's how we get confused.

Builder: How can you not know your enemies and friends? How can you be confused?

Senator: Words matter. That's all I can say.

Builder: Director, you know the truth about this.

Director: I do. And Senator is right. Words matter.

Builder: If you call a pig a horse, is it a horse?

Director: No, but you might come to think it is.

Builder: You might. But I? Never.

Director: But what if others come to think it's a horse? Will you disabuse them? Can you disabuse them without betraying the lie?

Builder: Betraying the lie. Count on you to put it that way.

Director: How would you have me put it?

Builder: The lie is a means, a tool.

Director: A tool to fool the supposed friend?

Builder: Yes.

Director: And how about your other friends?

Builder: What about them?

Director: Don't you have to fool them, too, to keep up the lie?

Builder: I suppose.

Director: Then tell us this. Do you agree that when you lie to someone you distance yourself?

Builder: And that's often good.

Director: Good when you distance yourself from friends?

Builder: Sometimes you have no choice.

Director: Tell us. Why would you keep an enemy close?

Builder: For the sake of revenge.

Director: And revenge must in, cost be damned?

Builder: Yes.

Senator: So, and no surprise, you value revenge above closeness with friends.

Builder: You want the truth? I never found a friend like the one I lost.

Senator: And you let that loss eat you alive.

— Recovery

Director: So it's all or nothing for you. A friend as good as the one you lost, or no friends at all.

Builder: How many people do you think have true friends?

Director: A friend like yours? Not too many. Most friendships are less intense.

Builder: You think we were too intense?

Director: Is that what people told you?

Builder: That's what my father said. He tried to keep us apart. And that's when it happened.

Director: The accident?

Builder: He killed himself.

Director: I'm sorry, Builder.

Senator: Your wound hasn't healed.

Builder: It hasn't. And it's been a long time. More than thirty years. This is the first time I've talked about it with anyone.

Senator: I hope it does you some good.

Builder: I think it is doing some good. And do you know why? No one is offering a shoulder to cry on.

Senator: What was it that philosopher said? You should offer yourself as a hard camp bed to your recovering friend.

Builder: Recovery. I never thought that was possible.

Director: What makes you think it might be now?

Builder: I know I want friends.

Senator: So you'll put them above revenge?

Builder: Yes, but it's not that simple.

Director: Why not?

Builder: I have a lifetime of habits to change.

Senator: Start the journey of a thousand miles with just one step.

Builder: Yes, Senator. That's good advice. And I've taken several steps here tonight.

Director: What do you think will be the hardest habit to break?

Builder: Hiding my true self.

Director: You want to make yourself known to all?

Builder: No, of course not all. To my friends. And they'll remind me who I am.

Senator: They'll keep you honest.

Builder: Yes.

Director: And what about revenge?

Builder: They'll help me with that, too.

— Forgetting

Senator: I think you should let your friends help you forget about revenge.

Builder: I can't do that, Senator.

Senator: Why not?

Builder: Because forgetting is the one great sin.

Senator: Remember your friend always. But your revenge does him no good. And doesn't do you any good, either.

Builder: Ah, but if you knew the satisfactions I've known....

Senator: Use your power for the good of your friends.

Builder: I'll do both. Work for the good of my friends, and for the harm of my enemies. That's the one true way.

Senator: I thought neither harm nor good was the one true way.

Builder: The one true way can change, depending on your perspective.

Senator: Director, can you talk some sense into him?

Director: He's talking sense already.

Senator: How so?

Director: Don't we all seek to help our friends and harm our enemies?

Senator: No, some of us love our enemies.

Builder: I think some of us say we love our enemies, while in fact we do them harm.

Senator: I'm not denying there are hypocrites out there. But some of us really do love.

Builder: Then you've got your heads in the clouds.

Director: How about a compromise here?

Senator: What have you got in mind?

Director: We destroy the bad in an enemy's soul, in order to bring out the good.

Builder: We harm and help at once? I like the destruction. But why assume there's good?

Senator: We all have some good somewhere.

Builder: I don't know about that. I've known some pretty rotten people. Haven't you?

Senator: Then you should simply destroy and hope for the best.

Builder: I can live with that. But without the hope.

Senator: The good will be there just the same. But you really shouldn't forget about hope. This is another step you need to take on your way to your friends.

Builder: Oh? Why?

Senator: Because there is no friendship without hope.

Builder: I don't understand.

Senator: Because friends need to look toward all three.

Builder: All three?

Senator: Past, present, and future.

Builder: And our hope is in the future.

Senator: Yes, but hope animates the present, and gains support from the past.

Builder: Not from my past. I want to forget much of my past, not have it bubble up into my present.

Senator: That's a mistake. We need to draw lessons from the past.

Builder: Then I'll draw the lessons and forget the rest—except for my friend. He stands apart, outside time, his spirit indelibly marking my soul.

— Souls

Director: How does his spirit mark your soul?

Builder: Through its power.

Director: And is that power... life?

Builder: That power is life itself.

Director: So the more power of spirit, of soul, the greater the life.

Builder: Yes.

Director: Can we build the strength of our souls, or are their powers fixed at birth?

Builder: I don't know. I only know power when I see it. You have a powerful soul.

Director: I don't know about that. But what about you?

Builder: My soul is very powerful.

Director: How do you know?

Builder: I have incredible drive.

Director: Why is it incredible?

Builder: Because it almost overwhelms me.

Director: Maybe your soul is too powerful.

Builder: If not powerful, what would you have it be?

Senator: Calm like the sea.

Builder: Yes, Senator, but the sea isn't always calm. And when it's not, it tosses the ships above.

Director: Who rides in those ships?

Builder: Fishers who'd catch my friends.

Director: Your friends?

Builder: Those I let swim in the truth of my soul.

Senator: So you drive the ships away.

Builder: No, that's not enough. I send them down.

Director: To see your deep truth?

Builder: What? No. To drown all aboard.

— Depths, Damage

Director: Your enemies all drown, but all your friends swim?

Builder: Yes.

Senator: But what does it mean to swim?

Builder: Oh, don't be too literal about the metaphor.

Director: That's good advice. But keeping loose, how is it for you with them?

Builder: What do you mean?

Director: When you swim in the truth of your friends' souls, do you stay near the surface?

Builder: No, I don't need to.

Director: You can breathe underwater?

Builder: Ha, ha. No, what I mean is this. When your depths are as deep as mine, you have no problem sounding the depths of another.

Director: Really?

Builder: Yes. But I have to say, a lifetime of observation has taught me not to expect too much by way of depth.

Senator: What do you expect of us?

Builder: You both have depths. But let's stop the metaphor here.

Senator: But what's behind the metaphor? You want to drown your enemies? What does that mean?

Builder: I want to bring them harm.

Director: What kind of harm?

Builder: Damage to the brain, the heart, the soul.

Director: But your enemies, aren't they already damaged? Or are you the enemy of the healthy and whole?

Builder: Count on you to ask me that.

Director: What's your answer?

Builder: I'm the enemy of the damaged.

Director: What causes the damage?

Builder: Who can say? You just know it when you see it.

Senator: But what if someone says you're damaged, too?

Builder: Then they're wrong. I'm healthy and whole in my power.

Senator: And if you lose your power one day?

Builder: Then you can gloat—and say I'm damaged, too.

— Persuasion

Senator: I don't want to gloat. I want to persuade you to heal.

Builder: Heal what?

Senator: Yourself and others. You need to use your power for this—or abandon it once and for all.

Director: What would it take to persuade you, Builder?

Builder: To heal or abandon? I would never abandon power, out of a sort of moral obligation.

Senator: Moral obligation. Ha, ha.

Builder: Laugh all you like, Senator. Do you deny that promises are moral?

Senator: They're moral when they're kept.

Builder: Well, I keep a promise to myself—never to throw power away.

Director: And do you promise you'll put it to good use?

Builder: Good as I see it, yes.

Director: But good-as-you-see-it implies you know not everyone thinks it's good.

Builder: Good and bad aren't always good and bad, if that's what you mean. We've been over this.

Director: Yes, but why not strive to clear things up?

Builder: How?

Director: You can say there's good and then there's seeming good, just as there's bad and seeming bad. Then explain in detail why each is so.

Senator: That would be a service to us all.

Builder: Bah.

Director: Why do you object?

Builder: Opinions will always differ.

Senator: But the difference between them is sometimes more and sometimes less.

Builder: You'd have me make it less?

Senator: And have us agree more than we do? I would.

Builder: But power can be used for so much more than agreement.

Senator: That's why it's often so bad.

— Good

Builder: Sometimes agreement takes force.

Senator: Of course that's what you think.

Builder: But force persuades. It's the only thing certain people understand.

Director: Those who only respect force, are they good?

Builder: No, I'd say they're bad.

Director: What do the good respect?

Senator: I'll tell you what they respect. Reason.

Director: Builder?

Builder: I agree. But Senator and I have different notions of what reason is.

Senator: What's reason to you?

Builder: Not-so-subtle suggestions about the disposition of various forces.

Senator: An analysis of power, you mean.

Builder: Yes, which happens to be an exercise of power itself. But not naked power. Reason is power fully clothed.

Director: Do you allow the naked in your armies?

Builder: I give them uniforms.

Senator: To cloak their power of reason?

Builder: Sometimes, yes. And sometimes to cloak their lack.

Senator: Those who lack reason, can they respect it?

Builder: Usually not.

Senator: So more often than not they're bad.

Builder: I'd rather say they're not good.

Senator: Not good, bad—there's no difference here. But do you tell them the truth?

Builder: That they're not good? I do. And they love it.

Senator: Because they know they're bad? But don't they want to be good?

Builder: You overrate the attraction of being good. Knowledge of good's limited appeal—has been the secret to my success.

— Reason

Director: Yes, but Senator, what do you say about reason? What's reason to you?

Senator: Reason is logic replete with facts.

Builder: And the most important facts involve power.

Senator: If that's all you can think of, you'll miss the point.

Builder: The point? How so?

Senator: We need all the facts, not just those related to power. Because logic with only some of the facts isn't always true.

Builder: Senator, it can take a lifetime to have all the facts.

Director: Then what must we do?

Builder: Reason with what we've got, then adjust when we learn more.

Director: How do we learn more? Through luck?

Builder: No! We use all the power we have to fight for the facts.

Director: Certain facts are no doubt worth the fight. But when we have them, and we've reasoned on them—what do we do?

Senator: We gently reason with the good.

Director: And if they won't listen?

Builder: Then they're no good. And so we force the facts on them.

Senator: And if someone of reason listens but disagrees with what we say? Do we force them, too?

Builder: Why would they disagree? We give them true facts then employ logic on them. What more do they want?

Senator: Some have to arrive on their own.

Builder: Yes, but when will they arrive? Do we wait all our lives for them to catch up?

Senator: Sometimes we do.

Director: What do we do while we wait?

Senator: Run a business, pursue philosophy, hold office—many things.

Director: And we'll do these things well because we have reason?

Senator: Yes, of course.

Director: But now I wonder. Does success always indicate reason?

Senator: Well, sometimes success is just luck.

Builder: And sometimes it's due to nothing but force.

Director: Doesn't reason at times dictate we succeed through force?

Builder: Of course it does—when reason fails.

Senator: Yes, but when it does, how do we know our reasoning wasn't bad?

Builder: That's simple. Our reasoning is bad if we don't get what we want. Don't you know what reasoning really is?

Senator: What is it?

Builder: Insisting on what you want. Logic and facts are deployed toward this end.

Senator: Again, you're cynical here.

Builder: Am I? Or maybe you don't know reason very well.

Senator: Director, what do you say about this?

Director: I don't have much to say.

Builder: When do you have much to say?

Director: When speaking from a different angle.

Builder: What angle?

Director: The angle of friends.

Builder: What do you mean?

Director: Haven't you noticed this? Those who love to reason long to reason with reasoned friends.

Senator: It's true.

Director: And if reason fails with your friends, does that diminish the longing?

Senator: Not at all. It makes the longing greater.

Director: So what do you do?

Senator: Learn to reason the best you can, and try again.

Builder: And if your reason fails again and again and again?

Senator: You might need to find yourself—some different friends.

— Benefits

Builder: What if your friends appreciate your reason?

Director: Then they're good friends. And you should treat them like silver.

Builder: Silver? Why not gold?

Director: Because you don't want to spoil them.

Senator: There's no spoiling a friend. The better you treat them, the better they'll treat you. And if they don't? They're not really your friend.

Builder: What does treating them better mean? You don't disagree with what they say?

Senator: You can disagree—but politely.

Builder: I see. And if you have power? Do you use it for their benefit?

Senator: Yes, of course. And they'll use their power to benefit you.

Builder: But what if your powers aren't nearly matched? One benefits more than the other?

Senator: Oh, why are you so worried about this? Don't you know it's a benefit to benefit a friend?

Builder: But the one with less power can't enjoy that benefit as much.

Senator: The friend with less power can always give love.

Director: Ah, love rescues us again. Builder, would you trade the fruits of power for love?

Builder: It depends whose love.

Senator: All love is good.

Builder: Even that of those who simply love my power?

Senator: But they're not your friends. Friends love you for what you are.

Builder: What am I but the power I've amassed?

Senator: You really are stuck on this, aren't you? You are what you love.

Builder: But what is love?

Senator: If you have to ask....

Builder: I do have to ask.

Director: Why?

Builder: Because so many things pass for love that aren't.

Director: You'd like to clear things up?

Builder: I would.

— Heart

Senator: If I were you, I wouldn't worry about setting others straight.

Builder: Why not?

Senator: Because you've got something more pressing.

Builder: What?

Senator: Your heart. I'm afraid it atrophied since you lost your friend.

Builder: And now I need to focus on making it strong?

Senator: Yes.

Director: But maybe his heart is strong already.

Senator: How? He hasn't loved anyone in all these years.

Director: How? Through love of power.

Senator: Director, I can't believe you want to make that point.

Director: Why? Power is hard to love. And if hard, a good workout for the heart.

Builder: Even I don't believe you mean that in earnest.

Director: Do you think power is easy to love?

Builder: I don't.

Director: What makes it hard?

Builder: It's hard to win and once you've won it, it imposes harsh demands.

Director: What's harder? To win power, or to win the heart of a friend? Tell us honestly, now.

Builder: I don't know.

Director: Think back to your friend. What did it take to win his heart?

Builder: It took nothing. Our hearts were simply one.

Director: So power was harder to win than the heart of your friend.

Senator: Director, what are you trying to say?

Director: I've said it.

Senator: But we don't believe you.

Director: What's to believe?

Senator: You're just teasing.

Director: I think you're making an assumption that's giving you trouble.

Senator: What assumption?

Director: That what's harder to win is more worthwhile. So you want friendship to be harder to win than power.

Senator: Isn't the harder more worthwhile?

Director: In this case? No.

Builder: You're recommending the easy way out?

Director: For you? Yes. I think you're too hard on yourself.

Senator: And if someone is too easy on themselves? Do what? Seek power?

Director: Yes.

Senator: This is ridiculous!

Director: I pride myself on being good for a laugh.

Builder: That's not what you pride yourself on. But let me tell you. Nothing is easier than to let power slip away.

Senator: I disagree. For someone like you, that's the hardest thing in the world. Power permeates your soul. It's in your every thought. It's in your every deed. Power is everything to you—well, almost everything. Is it easy to give all-but-everything up? No.

Director: Tell us, Senator. Do you think friendship and power don't mix?

Senator: Friendship and Builder's kind of power don't mix.

Director: So you're saying, basically, that friendship for Builder is the hardest thing in the world.

Senator: Yes.

Builder: I think you still worship the hard.

Senator: What I worship is innocence. There's nothing harder to maintain. And you should know—it takes a degree of innocence to win a true friend.

Builder: Then all my hopes are dashed.

Director: Because you're not innocent?

Builder: I tasted the forbidden fruit from the tree of power.

Director: And you were banished from paradise once you had?

Builder: I was banished well before I had knowledge of power. I was banished when I lost my friend.

Director: So the punishment was before the crime.

Builder: You're just trying to tempt me.

Director: To do what?

Builder: Think that since the 'punishment' drove me to lose my innocence, I am, in a way, still innocent.

Director: Maybe you are.

Builder: And if I am? What should I do?

Director: Let your knowledge win you some friends.

— Hard

Senator: Yes, but innocence lost is innocence lost.

Builder: That's true. And who of us hasn't lost innocence in life? Who is blameless? But how hard should we be on ourselves for that? Life is hard enough. I think you're too hard on yourself, Senator.

Senator: No, I don't think I am. I sometimes think I'm not hard enough.

Builder: But aren't the voters hard on you?

Senator: They can be very difficult, yes. But that's their right.

Builder: Whatever you mean by that, the point is that you have it hard. And you put yourself in this situation. So I'd say you're hard on yourself.

Senator: Maybe. But I still think I might not be hard enough.

Director: What does it mean to be hard enough?

Senator: It has to do with the responsible use of power.

Builder: Ha! If we're not hard enough we're irresponsible?

Senator: Yes.

Director: I'm not so sure being hard on ourselves makes us responsible.

Senator: What does?

Director: Knowing how to use power—and using it well.

Builder: Tell me, Director. What do I have to learn about the use of power?

Director: How to give it away and keep it at once.

Builder: What paradox is this?

Director: It's called sharing. But it's not what you think.

Builder: What should I think?

Director: That sharing means to open up.

Builder: Share the secrets of my power? And, what, I should hold nothing back?

Director: From your closest, most trustworthy friends? You tell me.

Builder: Ha, ha. You want to know the workings of my empire, beyond what you've already seen.

Director: I admit to curiosity. But Senator might have a real need to know.

Builder: And what's to stop him from turning on me once he knows?

Director: Your friendship. Or don't you think that's enough?

Builder: I'd be giving him the world in trust. What would he give me?

Senator: I don't want your world in trust.

Builder: What do you want?

Senator: Freedom—to do as I see fit.

— Fit

Builder: Fit concerning my world? We'll never be friends.

Director: Not so fast. What if what Senator sees fit isn't what you see fit?

Builder: That's my point!

Director: Yes, but isn't having power exactly that?

Builder: Exactly what?

Director: Having others do for you what you yourself can't.

Builder: Why can't I do it?

Director: Because you can't see how it needs to be done.

Builder: And Senator can? Okay. But it goes both ways.

Senator: I'm open to help.

Builder: Are you? Suppose I see that your career, your power, depends on something being done, something you don't think is right.

Senator: And you want me to do it? We'd agree to disagree.

Builder: But I as your friend would do something more.

Senator: What would you do?

Builder: I'd do the dirty deed—without your knowing.

Senator: Someone who does that isn't a friend.

Builder: You'd rather not succeed? You just have to be willing not to know.

Senator: Knowledge is power.

Builder: Not in this case, it isn't.

Senator: Director, what do you think about this?

Director: You want to keep your hands clean.

Senator: Of course I do.

Director: But Builder says that's not enough—and Builder might know.

Senator: He might. But you should know—if it comes down to it, I'm fine with losing power.

Builder: But I'd never be. And that's the difference between us.

— Support

Director: So you'd accept the dirty deed from a friend.

Builder: Of course I would. And I'd like to know all about it, too.

Director: Where will you find a friend like this?

Builder: I hope right here in you.

Director: Your hope is misplaced.

Builder: If Senator weren't here, I think you'd admit it's very well placed.

Director: You think Senator limits what I say?

Builder: I know he does.

Director: Senator, what do you think about that?

Builder: I don't believe I have that power over you.

Director: And I agree. I'm free, Builder, to say whatever I like.

Builder: Then say this. When you love a friend, are you willing to do whatever it takes to lend support?

Director: So long as it doesn't undermine what I love in my friend—and what my friend loves in me.

Senator: I couldn't have put it better.

Builder: Oh, forget about undermining. What's worth supporting in a friend?

Director: The life of the mind.

Builder: You'd share this life with your friend?

Director: There's nothing more worth sharing.

Builder: How do you share?

Director: We talk.

Builder: And it's as simple as that?

Director: As simple and plain as day.

Builder: But when you talk, sometimes you talk at night.

Senator: What's that supposed to mean?

Builder: Not all topics can stand the light, as we've said.

Director: What's such a topic for you, Builder?

Builder: The ways of power.

Director: That's too bad.

Builder: Why?

Director: Because then we can't talk about them.

Builder: Because you'd bring light?

Director: Yes. And so would you.

Builder: Well, maybe these things can stand a little light, a candle in the dark.

Senator: But we want much more than a little light here. We want the sun to shine in.

Builder: Is that what you want, Director? You want to flood my world with light?

Director: The only one who can flood your world, my friend—is you.

— Amoral

Builder: That's true. But you're just using one truth to hide another.

Director: What truth am I hiding?

Builder: The truth that if Senator weren't here, you'd sing a very different tune.

Senator: How so, Builder?

Builder: He'd admit he loves to talk about all the dark things. And he'd keep them where they belong—in the dark.

Director: Builder, do you really think I change what I say depending who's present?

Builder: I do. And you know I'm right.

Director: Then I should cling to Senator, and all my good friends, in order to stay honest.

Builder: So you'd never spend time on your own with me? What if you were forced to come alone to my office one day?

Director: I'd stick to the business before us and offer nothing more.

Builder: But what if I offered something more? Would you stop up your ears?

Director: I'd ask to leave.

Builder: But why? Are you afraid of me?

Director: I'm afraid for you.

Builder: For me? Again? What's to be afraid of now?

Senator: I know what. The continued corruption of your soul.

Builder: How is my soul corrupt?

Senator: Oh, Builder, you know about your soul. Every time you tell a lie, every time you do a dirty deed—your soul corrupts.

Builder: Maybe it's best to have no soul.

Director: But people without souls can't be friends.

Builder: You seem to like saying who can and can't be friends.

Director: I do like saying it—because I like to say what's true.

Senator: Director is right. He and I are friends because we both have healthy souls. You, however, don't.

Builder: But that's what makes me flexible. It leaves me unencumbered.

Senator: I'm afraid you'll always be alone.

Director: Not if he makes a stand.

Builder: Listen to you two. Senator, I know you make moral stands—because you can't get anything done in the senate! But you, Director? I think it's a bit more complicated.

Director: What can't I get done?

Builder: You can't be done with philosophy.

Director: I just can't stop loving all that wisdom I see? Do you agree it's wise to be moral?

Builder: No, I think just the opposite—as you know.

Director: So the wise are immoral, amoral?

Builder: Amoral, yes.

Director: And that gives them what? Flexibility?

Builder: Correct.

Director: But you can't be friends with the amoral.

Builder: I can't understand why you say this.

Senator: I can. It has to do with trust. We have to be able to trust our friends completely. If everyone is oh so flexible, how can we trust they'll not slip away from us like some eel?

Director: Or snake.

Senator: Precisely. At best the amoral can meet, acknowledge one another, and go their separate ways.

Builder: Listen to you! Acknowledge one another. It's much more than mere acknowledgement.

Director: What is it?

Builder: Love.

Senator: The amoral love the amoral?

Builder: It takes strength and courage to be amoral.

Senator: No, it takes strength and courage to be moral. Amorality takes... nothing!

Director: Tell us, Builder. Was your friend amoral?

Builder: We were young. We didn't think of ourselves that way.

Director: How did you think of yourselves?

Builder: As free.

Director: Were you free?

Builder: We were. But our freedom....

Director: What about your freedom?

Builder: It wasn't meant to last.

— Growth

Director: Does revenge last?

Builder: The memory of revenge can last the rest of your life.

Director: But for that the revenge must be high quality.

Builder: High quality revenge? Ha, ha. Sure. But what makes for quality?

Director: Growth.

Builder: What growth?

Director: The growth that comes of learning.

Builder: What am I supposed to learn?

Director: I wasn't thinking of you. I was thinking of the objects of your revenge.

Builder: All they need to do is suffer.

Director: But don't you know? The best revenge is having your victim learn and grow.

Builder: They learn what they did wrong?

Director: Yes.

Builder: That's fine. But why do I want them to grow?

Director: Growth is painful. Isn't that reason enough?

Builder: You're making some sense. But what if they learn but don't grow?

Director: Growth almost always follows learning, and often in ways you can't imagine.

Builder: But growth is good. Why do I want something good for them?

Director: Think of yourself as a teacher.

Builder: A teacher?

Director: A teacher's best revenge against unruly students is when they learn and grow.

Builder: But aren't the students happy when they have?

Director: They are.

Builder: So you want me to make the objects of my revenge happy? You can't be serious. Besides, this will never work.

Director: Why not?

Builder: The people I deal with are beyond repair.

Director: How can you tell?

Builder: They're not open to things.

Director: What things?

Builder: Things outside their narrow interests.

Director: And you, you're open to these sorts of things?

Builder: Of course I am. I'm talking to you two here tonight, aren't I?

Senator: You don't think talking to us is in your narrow interest?

Builder: Tomorrow I go before the board and fight for a permit for my tallest building yet. That's my narrow interest. And you can't help me here. Or do you think you can?

Senator: No, I can't help you there. Director?

Director: I'm too far removed to know what I can or can't do.

Builder: You want me to bring you in? Come with me tomorrow and see. Maybe you'll have some good suggestions.

Director: And if I don't have any?

Builder: I still could use... the company.

— Useful

Director: Tell us something. If the board gives you the permit, is it good?

Builder: A good board? Yes, I'd say it's good.

Director: And if it doesn't give you the permit, it's bad?

Builder: Very.

Senator: That seems a little too easy, don't you think? What if they give you the permit because you bribe them? Good people?

Builder: Sure.

Senator: Be serious.

Builder: Alright. Maybe they're more useful than good.

Senator: And you'd rather surround yourself with the useful than the good?

Builder: If you're not useful, what good are you to me?

Senator: Yes, but the useful themselves can be good or bad.

Builder: Then I prefer the useful good.

Director: What's the difference between the two?

Builder: Loyalty. The bad will turn on you given good opportunity. The good? They'll think twice.

Director: So you have to recognize when someone is thinking of turning on you.

Builder: Yes, and that's much easier with the honest.

Director: Why?

Builder: Because they have no skill in deceit. You can see when something is wrong with them. Not so with the others.

Senator: So you value openness.

Builder: Yes.

Senator: And yet you yourself are closed.

Builder: I don't want my enemies to know what I'm thinking.

Director: Which makes you very hard to persuade.

Builder: Why do you care about that?

Director: Because that's what friends do. They persuade one another.

Builder: To do what? Act in each other's interest?

Director: Do you see anything wrong with that?

Builder: It's not that simple.

Senator: Why wouldn't it be? If you're open with each other about your interests, it should be easy to help—or easier, at least.

Builder: You don't understand the needs of power.

Senator: What's to understand?

Builder: Its ways are dark, solitary.

Senator: How do you know?

Builder: How do I know? I live this every day!

Senator: Maybe you're in a deep rut. Have you ever considered that?

Builder: A rut of power and success? Please.

Senator: With all your power and success, can't you afford a little experimentation?

Builder: What would you have me do? Get out of my rut and discover something I already know?

Senator: You're not open to discovery?

Builder: Let's say I am. And I discover power is other than I think. What do I do?

Senator: Change your ways.

Builder: Just like that? Snap my fingers and it's done? Oh, Senator. It's not so simple—when you're in deep.

— Getting Out

Senator: Then find the friends who can help pull you out.

Builder: And do what when they have? Come work for you?

Senator: Just live off your wealth.

Builder: Again, and do what? Collect stamps?

Senator: What's wrong with collecting stamps?

Builder: Look, without my empire to run I'd go mad.

Director: Then run it differently.

Builder: How?

Director: So good friends feel comfortable coming to work with you.

Builder: But it's not about comfort.

Director: What's it about?

Builder: Victory, and whatever it takes. Are you going to tell me to give up victories in order to work with friends?

Director: Find friends who love victory, too.

Builder: Don't you?

Director: I like to win.

Builder: Yes, but do you love it? Do long for it in your soul?

Director: No, not like that.

Builder: Why not?

Director: Because I have philosophy.

Builder: Philosophy doesn't give you victories in argument?

Director: I'm not looking for that.

Builder: Then what are you looking for?

Director: Truth.

Builder: And if you lose, how much truth is there for you then?

Director: Sometimes lots, as I've said.

Builder: You learn all the more that way? You're just saying that.

Director: Let me put it this way. Sometimes when I philosophize with others I'm reduced to silence. Most would consider that a loss. But in my silence I see. I see the truth.

Builder: And?

Director: I'm satisfied.

Builder: Okay. But let's get back to the point. How do I find a way out?

Director: Out begins within.

Builder: Yes, but in begins without.

Senator: Does it? Does the world make us, or do we make the world?

Builder: Both. Once we're made, forced to be what we are, we turn on the world.

Senator: And make it in our own image?

Builder: No. Then the cycle never ends. We must be creative with the world.

Director: What does that mean? The world is our canvas?

Builder: Yes. And we can decide to paint in gentle little strokes, or we can splash color all around.

Director: Let me guess. You like to splash.

Builder: Yes. I want the world to be other than it would otherwise be.

Senator: But gentle strokes can accomplish that. You just have to be patient.

Builder: Yes, but the gentle are often too gentle. They can learn a thing or two from a splasher like me.

Senator: But splashing chases the gentle away.

Builder: Then we'll invite them in when the splashing is done.

Director: To do what? Paint over the worst of the splashes?

Builder: The splashers won't like that, you know.

Director: But will they even notice? They splash, and move on to the next big thing.

Builder: Yes, but I would notice.

Director: You?

Builder: Why do you sound surprised?

Director: Because you're impatient.

— Beauty

Senator: And you know what that means, don't you?

Builder: Tell me.

Senator: You don't have much love for the gentle.

Builder: Because it takes patience to love them?

Senator: Yes.

Builder: But how do you know I don't love them?

Senator: If you did, you'd bring more of them in.

Builder: To work their fine work?

Senator: Yes, on the canvases you provide.

Builder: What canvases?

Senator: Have you forgotten them? Your buildings! They're the greatest splashes of all.

Builder: Fine work is expensive, you know.

Senator: Yes, but beauty is worth it.

Builder: Who can argue against beauty and win? But the expense will be wasted on most.

Director: Will it? But why worry about those who can't appreciate beauty?

Senator: Director, don't be so quick to judge. Tastes vary. Just because some might not find beauty here, that doesn't mean they have no love for other beautiful things.

Director: Ah, thank you for not letting me get carried away.

Builder: It's good to get carried away in the cause of a friend.

Senator: It's never good to get carried away.

Builder: Oh, but it is. And that's how I'll choose my friends. I want them to get carried away in what I create. I want them to get carried away—in me.

Director: But what if your soul is still ugly?

Builder: What do you mean?

Director: You're not yet done with revenge.

Builder: You don't think there can be beautiful revenge? Delicate revenge? Revenge with taste?

Director: I'd have to see it. What does it involve?

Builder: Getting your enemy to swallow the truth.

Senator: All at once?

Builder: No, a bite at a time.

Senator: A bite is hardly revenge.

Builder: But over time? Many bites will change their way of thinking. Many bites will make them grow.

Director: And if they refuse to swallow even the tiniest morsel?

Builder: Then the revenge becomes... a little more rough.

— Sensitive

Senator: But you'll avoid the rough way if you can?

Builder: Yes, even though people will laugh at my change of heart.

Senator: Change of heart? You still want revenge.

Builder: Yes, but they won't appreciate my new means.

Senator: They'll think you've gone soft? But would you really let that stop you?

Builder: No, but it will take some time to adjust.

Director: To your new longing for revenge?

Builder: What new longing?

Director: For revenge on those who laugh.

Senator: You'll just have to get over that, Builder.

Builder: You think I'm too sensitive?

Director: There's no such thing as too sensitive—when you're sensitive at the right time.

Builder: What time?

Director: When you judge.

Builder: Judge?

Director: Others. Be sensitive when dealing with the sensitive, and less so with the rest.

Builder: And if they're not sensitive at all?

Director: Then you know what to do.

Senator: Yes, but first we have to ask—is it possible to make the insensitive sensitive?

Builder: What? What are you asking? If it's possible to make a stone come to life?

Director: You can wake someone up. And then they're sensitive to things they weren't aware of before.

Builder: Yes, but they have to be sensitive to begin with, or they'd never wake up.

Senator: So we just give up on the insensitive?

Builder: I'd be the first to celebrate their coming around. But I've never seen it happen.

Senator: But can't philosophy do something?

Director: It can only awaken the predisposed.

Senator: How do you know who's predisposed?

Director: The predisposed listen.

Builder: But those who hate philosophy will listen, too.

Senator: So there's listening, and then there's listening. Should philosophy silence itself toward those who hate?

Builder: No. Let philosophy show its power for all to see.

Senator: And when the haters do what they do best?

Builder: Refer them to me.

— Protection

Director: What kind of protection can you offer?

Builder: The only kind that matters. Physical protection.

Senator: You think it will come to that?

Builder: It has before. And I know why it happens.

Director: Oh? Please tell us.

Builder: Philosophy provokes.

Director: Intentionally or unintentionally?

Builder: Which is better?

Senator: Are you asking seriously?

Builder: I am.

Director: Why would philosophy intentionally provoke?

Builder: Because it's trying to wake someone up. As you've been trying with me.

Senator: We want to wake you up from your dream of revenge.

Builder: And substitute philosophy. Well, before I take the plunge, let me ask. Philosophy questions, right?

Director: It does.

Builder: Is there any limit to its questioning?

Director: Are you asking if it's limited by good sense?

Builder: Is it?

Senator: Of course it is.

Builder: Is it good sense when the questions annoy?

Director: Why do you ask?

Builder: I want to annoy my enemies no end. Questions are the means.

Director: Do you think that's what I do?

Builder: What do you do?

Director: Something more productive.

Builder: You don't try to awaken your enemies?

Senator: Philosophy should try to wake everyone up, friends and enemies alike.

Builder: But especially enemies. After all, if you're sound asleep, and someone wakes you up, are you happy with them?

Senator: No, you're annoyed.

Builder: And that's what I want my enemies to be.

Director: But won't they roll over and go back to sleep?

Builder: Yes, and I can wake them again and again and again. And I can do this every single day.

Director: You'll be wasting your time. But let me ask you something. If you wake someone up, and they're upset, and they come after you—what do you do?

Builder: I use my power to protect myself.

Director: Now, you see, I don't have power like yours. How do you think I protect myself?

Builder: You're a fast runner?

Director: No, I only attempt to awaken those I think can and want to wake up.

Builder: You mean, those who have nightmares?

Director: I mean, those who long for the day—and its light.

— Enemies

Builder: Then that's where I'll use my power.

Director: Power won't help you here.

Builder: Why not?

Director: What will you do? Power the sleeper awake?

Builder: You're saying my power is useless?

Director: As far as philosophy goes? Yes.

Builder: But people listen to me.

Director: The people who listen to you because you have power will be the first to stop their ears if you start talking philosophy.

Builder: But why?

Director: Because to them philosophy is a sign of weakness. It shows you have doubts. The powerful, to them, can have no doubts.

Builder: Well, you might have a point about doubts. But I want them to doubt, not me.

Director: Yes, but it doesn't work that way. If you never doubt, you have no business playing the philosopher.

Builder: So what are we saying? It's philosophy or power? Either or? I don't believe it.

Director: It can be philosophy and power both, if you know what you're doing.

Builder: What should I be doing?

Director: Talking to those who are already awake.

Builder: They'll talk philosophy with me?

Director: They will. Because they'll see you need training.

Builder: But, Director, why can't I get my training from you?

Director: I can give you some, but not enough. You need to learn to listen to others.

Builder: So I can grow.

Senator: Don't you want to grow?

Builder: I want to learn ways to deal effectively with my enemies. That's the growth I need.

Senator: I think you need to grow in how you understand your enemies.

Builder: What do you mean?

Senator: Your notion of who the enemy is might change.

Builder: Ha! What do you know about enemies? You think I don't know who my enemies are?

Senator: Some of your enemies are awake.

Builder: And how would you know?

Senator: I'm thinking of the odds. Most people can't be asleep.

Builder: I don't know about that.

Director: I met some of your enemies when I was working for you.

Builder: Were they 'most people'?

Director: I don't know. But we had several good talks.

Builder: You gave comfort to the enemy?

Senator: Builder, I don't like your use of 'comfort to the enemy'.

Builder: Why not?

Senator: It implies your workers owe you an allegiance like the one they owe to their country.

Builder: And they do. Ha, ha. I expect nothing less.

Senator: That has to stop if you hope to invite philosophy in.

Builder: They owe me no loyalty? I pay their bills!

Senator: The kind of loyalty you're talking about only has one object. Our nation. I'm loyal to that above all else. Are you?

Builder: I knew it would come to this. You question my loyalty. Don't you know what my empire does for this country?

Director: It pays great taxes?

Builder: Taxes, sure. But look at the buildings! Our skylines are filled with them. They make us great.

Senator: I don't know that they make us great. They might reflect our greatness.

Director: So long as...

Builder: What?

Director: ...they're not filled with those who are hardly awake.

— Philosophy 2

Builder: Yes, but I'm wondering something now.

Director: What are you wondering?

Builder: Whether we've really said what philosophy is.

Director: Why do you doubt?

Builder: Because I don't think it's as simple as waking others.

Director: What else would it be?

Builder: Getting others to think what you want.

Director: Do you think that's what I want?

Builder: I'm not sure. I have my doubts.

Director: How would I go about getting someone to think my way?

Builder: You could write a treatise.

Director: I haven't done that.

Builder: You could teach a certain set of principles to all who'll listen.

Director: I haven't done that, either.

Builder: You could knock out all their arguments so only yours remain.

Director: I'm the first to question the strength of any argument I make.

Builder: So it's true? Philosophers really just wake others up?

Director: Yes, but there's a problem.

Builder: What problem?

Director: What if the philosophers aren't awake?

Builder: They have to be conscious they might be asleep? I suppose there's truth in that. So we'll be wary. But, Director, now I want to say what I want.

Director: What do you want?

Builder: For you to work for me.

Director: You want me to harass your enemies?

Builder: I want you to help find those in my empire who want to wake up.

Director: And you're hoping that if you work with me for a while, you'll be able to do it on your own?

Builder: Yes.

Director: That's a tempting offer.

Senator: But, Builder, how much will he get paid?

Builder: As much as you get paid. Does that sound fair?

Senator: Of course it's not fair. Give him a bonus. You know, so much for each soul saved.

Builder: Ha, ha. Souls saved. That's good. Yes, we'll put a price on each head. What amount seems right? Director?

Director: I have no idea.

Senator: But I do. For each one saved give him his salary again.

Builder: Consider it done. And I think it's cheap, at that.

— End

Senator: What will you do with all the souls saved?

Builder: Do? They'll do the doing themselves.

Senator: And if some of them leave your employ? Are you open to that?

Builder: I am. It's good to have allies elsewhere.

Director: Indeed. Though not as good as you might think.

Builder: What do you mean?

Director: They'll be caught up in philosophy's work on their own. They won't have much time for us.

Builder: Well, I suppose that's just how it has to be.

Senator: You can really accept that? You who were so keen on loyalty just a few moments ago?

Builder: When it comes to philosophers, I expect loyalty to the cause, not me.

Senator: That's an improvement. But let's be clear. What's the cause?

Builder: Philosophy.

Director: And when philosophy calls me away from you?

Builder: As long as I've had the chance to learn what I can? I'll miss you, but I'll understand.

Director: And to think...

Builder: What?

Director: ...your friend brought you to this.

Builder: My friend? What about my friend?

Director: Your longing for your friend seems to have made you into a philosopher.

Builder: Yes, I know what you mean. And I also know the weight of your 'seems'.

Director: Then prove me wrong about 'seems'.

Builder: I have every intention to.

Senator: So where does that leave us tonight?

Director: It leaves us feeling it's time to go home.

Builder: Home. Philosophy can take us there. Can't it?

Director: It can. But if it doesn't? There's always revenge.

Builder: You shouldn't joke like that.

Director: You'll have to bear bad jokes, if you want to be a philosopher.

Builder: Why?

Director: Because you'll be misunderstood as an object of fun.

Builder: How will I be properly understood?

Director: As someone not overly concerned with 'properly'.

Builder: But that can't be all.

Director: No, but it will often take great effort to make yourself understood. And even then.... Does that discourage you?

Builder: No.

Senator: Well, I understand you better after tonight. I got the sense you were really trying, my friend—more so than I've ever seen you before.

Builder: Yes, but tell me. Are we really friends?

Senator: Of course we are!

Builder: Then maybe you can help me from time to time?

Senator: But I'm no philosopher.

Builder: True. But philosophy can't live on philosophy alone.

Senator: What does philosophy need from me?

Builder: Help seeing what it can't see.

Director: What can't philosophy see?

Builder: For instance? What happened here tonight. I didn't see it coming. Did you?

Director: See that I'd be offered a job? No, I never saw that. Did you see it, Senator?

Senator: I had a feeling you would.

Builder: Oh, you two know that's not what I'm talking about. I'm talking about the change in me!

Director: What changed?

Builder: You're just giving me a hard time. That's fine. I suppose I deserve it. So you really didn't know I'd change?

Director: I really didn't know. I can only see things as they unfold, not before.

Senator: It can take a long time for things to unfold.

Director: That's why we look to more than one thing.

Builder: Yes, but look at the time! We have a big day ahead.

Director: You still want me to come?

Builder: I do. And who knows? We might wake someone up!

Senator: If you had to choose between your permit and waking someone up, which would it be?

Builder: It won't come to that.

Senator: But if it did?

Builder: I would get the permit, and Director would do the waking. You see? We make a good team.

Director: We'd be a better team if we kept our priorities straight.

Builder: How are they not straight? Business is the necessity. Philosophy is the ideal.

Director: But, Builder, philosophy is my necessity. Business is simply a means. But you see business that way, don't you?

Builder: As means for power and revenge? Yes.

Senator: And also as means for friends.

Builder: Yes, of course—for friends, too.

Director: Friends. How do friends and philosophy relate?

Builder: There are no true friends without philosophy. And there is no true philosophy without friends.

Director: Do you really mean it?

Builder: I really do.

Senator: Well, on that note let's say goodnight. And what a night it's been! You opened up at last.

Director: Not only did Builder come out of his isolation—he took a step toward philosophy.

Builder: Only a step?

Director: Just a step. And there are more steps to take. So you have to be patient.

Builder: But why not take all the steps right now? I'm ready.

Director: It doesn't work that way. You need some time to understand the step you took.

Builder: How much time?

Director: Time enough to ensure you don't turn back.

Builder: What do you mean?

Director: If you rush, you'll likely be overwhelmed.

Builder: And I'll turn back? What happens if I turn back?

Director: You'll live a double lie.

Builder: What double lie?

Director: The lie you tell others about who you are.

Builder: But that's just one lie. What's the other?

Director: The lie you tell yourself about the same.

Builder: What if I don't try to go back but stop going forward?

Director: A natural pressure will urge you onward again.

Builder: And if I resist?

Director: What do you think happens when we resist nature?

Builder: Nothing good. But where does this natural pressure lead?

Director: To a point where philosophy possesses your passion.

Builder: And what does it do with my passion? Snuff it out, so I'm some cold logic machine?

Director: No. Philosophy amplifies your passion and returns it to you.

Builder: I never thought of philosophy as having to do with passion before.

Director: That's because philosophers must learn to temper their passion.

Builder: Why?

Director: Because they want philosophy to grow.

Senator: Director, what good comes of philosophy's growth?

Director: I have to speak truth to you here. I don't know.

Builder: You don't know? Of course you know!

Director: Look at it this way. If I'm a doctor, I can set a broken leg. But I can't know where my patient will walk when it heals.

Builder: But in the case of philosophy, healed patients will go on to heal other patients.

Director: Yes, though there's no guarantee.

Builder: What do you mean?

Director: A philosopher-doctor might go their whole life and never heal a single soul.

Builder: Or they might heal many.

Director: True. It all depends. So you have to be prepared.

Builder: What do you do if you never heal?

Director: You might leave behind a legacy.

Builder: Writings, you mean?

Director: Writings, sure. And non-written deeds.

Builder: But what if people don't understand them for what they are?

Senator: Someone certainly will, eventually. That's the indispensable hope.

Director: And with that we say goodnight. Builder and I need some rest. We have a big day before us.

Builder: We do, though I don't feel much like sleep. I'll stay up and think about all we said, and what it means. And that will help prepare me for... tomorrow.

Printed in the United States
By Bookmasters